Competitive Intelligence

FINANCIAL TIMES

In an increasingly competitive world, we believe it's
quality of thinking that will give you the edge – an idea
that opens new doors, a technique that solves a problem, or
an insight that simply makes sense of it all. The more you
know, the smarter and faster you can go.

That's why we work with the best minds in business
and finance to bring cutting-edge thinking and best
learning practice to a global market.

Under a range of leading imprints, including
Financial Times Prentice Hall, we create world-class
print publications and electronic products bringing our
readers knowledge, skills and understanding which can
be applied whether studying or at work.

To find out more about our business publications, or tell
us about the books you'd like to find, you can visit us at
www.business-minds.com

For other Pearson Education publications, visit
www.pearsoned-ema.com

Competitive Intelligence

How to acquire and use corporate intelligence and counter-intelligence

DOUGLAS BERNHARDT

 Prentice Hall
FINANCIAL TIMES

An imprint of Pearson Education

London ■ New York ■ Toronto ■ Sydney ■ Tokyo ■ Singapore ■ Hong Kong ■ Cape Town
New Delhi ■ Madrid ■ Paris ■ Amsterdam ■ Munich ■ Milan ■ Stockholm

PEARSON EDUCATION LIMITED

Head Office:
Edinburgh Gate
Harlow CM20 2JE
Tel: +44 (0)1279 623623
Fax: +44 (0)1279 431059

London Office:
128 Long Acre
London WC2E 9AN
Tel: +44 (0)20 7447 2000
Fax: +44 (0)20 7447 2170
Website: www.briefingzone.com
          www.Business-minds.com

First published in Great Britain in 2003

ISBN 0 273 65928 6

British Library Cataloguing in Publication Data
A CIP catalogue record for this book can be obtained from the British Library.

10 9 8 7 6 5 4 3 2 1

Typeset by Monolith – www.monolith.uk.com
Printed and bound in Great Britain by Ashford Colour Press Ltd, Gosport, Hants.

The Publishers' policy is to use paper manufactured from sustainable forests.

About the author

Douglas Bernhardt is a Director of the Geneva-based consultancy iMentor Management Consulting SA. iMentor's service lines include consulting and executive education in competitive strategy, business intelligence and corporate counterintelligence for companies in a wide array of industry sectors. Previously, Douglas co-founded, and for seven years ran, a leading European competitive intelligence research practice in Geneva and London.

Douglas teaches the subject of business intelligence as part of the MBA programmes at Thunderbird – The American Graduate School of International Management (French-Geneva campus), the Graduate School of Business, University of Cape Town, and other leading business schools. He also lectures on the subject of competitive intelligence as part of an advanced marketing training programme for a major Swiss pharmaceutical company.

Douglas is the author of the book *Perfectly Legal Competitor Intelligence: How to Get It, Use It and Profit from It* (London: Financial Times/Pitman, 1993) and *Competitive Intelligence in Pharmaceuticals: The Strategic Advantage* (London: Vision In Business, 1999). His articles have been published in numerous journals, including *Competitive Intelligence Review* (the official journal of SCIP – the Society of Competitive Intelligence Professionals) and *Long Range Planning* (the journal of the UK's Strategic Planning Society). He is a contributing author to two other important works: *The Art and Science of Business Intelligence Analysis* (Greenwich, CT: JAI Press, 1996) and *Managing Technology for Competitive Advantage* (London: Cartermill International/FT, 1997).

Douglas was a member of the SCIP board of directors from 1996 to 1999. His professional background includes the defence industry and foreign trade.

An American citizen, Douglas has lived in Europe for over 30 years. He was educated in the United States, Switzerland and the Panama Canal Zone.

Douglas Bernhardt can be contacted at:

iMentor Management Consulting SA
World Trade Centre II
CP 896
1215 Geneva 15
Switzerland

E-mail: dbernhardt@iMentorManagement.com

Dedicated to my children – Kimberly, Annabel, William and 'Claire' – who, like others of their generation, are the custodians of our future.

Contents

Appendices

References

Acknowledgements

Although this book is essentially the work of one author – with all the limitations this must inevitably involve – it is, in practice, the product of the enthusiasm, the experience, and the thinking of many others. I am especially grateful to Steve Whitehead, a friend and colleague in South Africa, for having contributed Chapter 9 on the important subject of counterintelligence. In addition, there are scores of others to whom I owe an enormous intellectual debt; one which can never be fully repaid. These include colleagues in Europe, South Africa, the United States, and elsewhere, employees, executives at client firms, students and scholars in the field of intelligence. Some of those who have been especially, if often unwittingly, helpful in sharpening my thinking on the twin disciplines of competitive intelligence and counterintelligence include Bill DeGenaro, Ben Gilad, Jan Herring, Paul Kinsinger, John Nolan, and Ken Sawka – many of their ideas are represented in the pages that follow.

Writing may be a solitary activity, but few authors live in a vacuum. My children know that 'Daddy writes things about business', and seem pleased that at least something – however esoteric – results from my time at the laptop. Friends, particularly those in that most magical of countries, South Africa, often wonder why I spend otherwise glorious days inside during my visits there, struggling, they politely observe, to construct just a few paragraphs; but they nevertheless encourage me, and remain ready to invite me to their evening braais.

Inspiration, of course, springs from many sources, but especially from people. The encouragement and welcome humour of close and knowledgeable friends such as Steve Delia, a former soldier in a regiment 'one must not name', and now an accomplished practitioner in the art of operational security, and Anja Kober, an exceptionally bright, dedicated practitioner in European competitive intelligence, have been especially important to me. There is also one special person in Finland whose insight, advice, and encouragement at the start of this project I shall always regard as invaluable, and who I shall never forget.

It would be an unforgivable omission if I were not to acknowledge my gratitude to the Society of Competitive Intelligence Professionals (SCIP). I have, for over twelve years, benefited greatly from the educational and 'networking' platforms provided by this unique organisation. I also had the privilege of serving for three years on its board of directors. SCIP's forums and publications are critically important to competitive intelligence professionals everywhere, and in turn to the corporate leaders that depend upon their output. I for one cannot imagine having refined my chosen craft as effectively, or as readily, without access to this important resource.

And last, I wish to express a special appreciation to Stephen Partridge, Senior Acquisitions Editor at Pearson Education. It was he who bravely gave the 'green light' to go ahead with this endeavour, and who, always with remarkable diplomacy, gave me the direction, or 'steers', I needed to stay on track, and prevent this document from becoming 'too academic'.

Introduction

To suggest that today's executive struggles in an environment characterized by perpetual change and uncertainty is, perhaps, stating the obvious. External forces seem to conspire to disrupt or impede even 'the best laid plans', which in turn cause both operational and 'political' turmoil inside even the bluest of 'blue-chip' companies. Nothing is as it was, and nothing is at it seems.

Never before has the need been greater for managers to understand the threats their organizations face, as well as the complex array of other forces likely to have a material impact on their business objectives and performance. And never before has it been as evident to all concerned that executives must anticipate and respond to these forces in order to reconcile them with their organizational responsibilities. But how do corporate leaders respond to threats of which they are either unaware or do not fully understand?

The challenges and risks faced by modern managers are in many respects little different from those which government policy-makers confront. Whereas political decision-makers have long relied upon their intelligence agencies to guide, or at least clarify, their thinking with unique evidence and analysis, most executives have little or no experience with the process or products of intelligence. Managers for the most part operate in an intelligence vacuum, relying upon their personal networks of information sources and, more dangerously, a wide array of unchallenged assumptions about their companies, their industries and their markets. And rarely does one find a manager able to answer the questions: what are our competitors trying to discover about us? and how are they doing it?

This book will equip managers with the necessary frameworks to:

- develop a clear understanding of the role and value of intelligence in all elements of the strategy process of their organizations;
- initiate the creation or upgrading of in-house intelligence and counterintelligence programmes;
- identify and define key intelligence topics (the firm's changing intelligence needs and priorities);
- use intelligence 'products' to help minimize risk and achieve competitive advantage;
- distinguish between tactical and strategic intelligence, and in turn better appreciate the critical differences between operational effectiveness and strategic positioning.

We cover in this book what are generally considered the core aspects of the competitive intelligence discipline. We revisit the issue of strategy. We consider the nature and role of intelligence as an integrated factor of the strategy process of firms. We set out the framework of 'key intelligence topics', the means by which firms identify their intelligence needs. We discuss the importance of a 'strategic early warning system' for minimizing risk and, thereby, augmenting corporate security. We cover the so-called 'intelligence cycle', and the 'products' which represent the output of that process. We suggest what companies should do to set up or upgrade their own internal intelligence function. We address the question of ethics. And we introduce the topic of counterintelligence.

This is a briefing document, not a textbook or training manual. There are many other 'weightier' works on the subject produced for intelligence practitioners. We have elected to examine those things which executives must know in order to be able to understand what competitive intelligence is, its bottom-line benefits, and just what it can and cannot do for them and their companies, hopefully providing just the right amount of transparency regarding a subject about which there are far too many misconceptions. Thus, at a time when the dot.com world of economic fantasy has all but vanished and firms find themselves under renewed pressures to consistently deliver superior returns, this briefing offers managers an invaluable tool for smarter decision-making and improved risk management.

Executive summary

Business has always been about competition: competition for customers, competition for markets and, ultimately, competition for superior returns. But today things are different. Over the past two decades or so the notion of globalization – a euphemism, we would argue, for hypercompetition of global proportions – has evolved from concept to universal reality. While new business opportunities emerge at a faster rate than at any time before, so too do the nature and extent of threats that companies, and indeed national economies, everywhere now face. While it is true that virtually no market or customer segment is beyond reach, neither is any business – no matter how big, powerful or well protected by its home nation – immune from 'surprise attack' or even defeat. Thus information, or intelligence, about rivals – their capabilities, their intentions, their future plans and their fundamental weaknesses – has become as indispensable to corporations as any of the traditional 'factors of production' (land, labour and capital).

In this book we address the key issues of intelligence that are – or should be – of greatest concern to corporate policy-makers. To begin with, we suggest that intelligence represents the 'flip side' of the strategy coin, that strategy without intelligence isn't strategy, it's guessing. We further argue that strategic intelligence is the sine qua non of 'intelligent strategy', and that the most important role for a dedicated intelligence support function is on the strategy stage.

Next we explore the specific roles that intelligence plays in the strategy process of the firm, the overarching process that underpins a company's strategy development and action. We also explain how and why the scope of competitive intelligence activities extends well beyond the boundaries of market research and how in each phase of the strategy process it adds value.

In Chapter 3 we consider how executives should think about their intelligence requirements, and decide what they really need and should expect from their intelligence staffs. We introduce the 'key intelligence topics' process, a framework that enables executives together with their intelligence personnel to identify the organization's intelligence priorities and provide a basis for operational planning and action.

We then cover the subject of strategic warning, and specifically the 'strategic early warning system' (SEWS), the means by which companies anticipate, detect and where possible prevent, or at least mitigate, strategic surprise. We explain what executives must expect from a warning 'product' or judgment, and describe the characteristics of the warning process.

Chapter 5 deals with intelligence as activity and offers a review of the intelligence cycle and its five interdependent steps or phases: planning and direction; collection;

processing and exploitation; analysis and production; and dissemination. Each phase in the process is examined in detail sufficient to enable executives to understand how the intelligence process works in practice, and thus what it is that needs to be managed.

In the chapter that follows we discuss the categories and characteristics of finished intelligence 'products', the deliverables which serve as the actionable instruments for management decision-making. We define and describe five types of intelligence products: current, estimative, research, science and technology, and warning.

Chapter 7 deals with intelligence as organization, that is the organizational mechanism or means by which intelligence is systematically collected, processed, analysed and disseminated to corporate management and staffs. Generic models of intelligence architecture are shown, and suggestions for setting up or upgrading a company's intelligence programme are discussed.

No work on competitive intelligence would be complete without reference to the issue of ethics. In Chapter 8 we remind the reader that the importance of ethics, in particular as it relates to the practice of competitive intelligence, is not to be underestimated. Intelligence activities undertaken without regard to the firm's ethical policies and guidelines are, at best, a one-way ticket to public embarrassment, and at worst an invitation to costly litigation.

Perhaps the least understood aspect of intelligence is that of counterintelligence. In Chapter 9 we offer a working definition of corporate counterintelligence as that aspect of intelligence covering all activity which is devoted to eliminating or reducing the effectiveness of rivals' intelligence operations, and to the protection of proprietary information against economic and industrial espionage. Most companies devote little attention to this aspect of intelligence operations, and what efforts they do make are largely ineffective. Executives seldom possess an ongoing understanding of what competitors and other 'interested parties' are trying to discover about them, why they're after it or how they're trying to do it. This final chapter focuses on the dangers of 'hostile' intelligence operations, and how companies should begin to think about better protecting their proprietary information.

Some say business is a game. Perhaps. We, on the other hand, regard it as a form of economic warfare, where the fruits of success include jobs, prosperity and general social stability and well-being, and conversely where 'casualties' range from jailed CEOs to disillusioned armies of unemployed and the economic and political disruption this can cause. Thus in business, as in warfare, intelligence must serve as 'the sword and the shield' of successful enterprises everywhere, providing management with the actionable information they need to make winning, profitable decisions.

List of abbreviations

ASIS	American Society for Industrial Security
BD&L	business development and licensing
BECCA	Business Espionage Controls and Countermeasures Association
BI	business intelligence
CDB	CEO's daily brief
CEO	chief executive officer
CI	competitive intelligence
CIA	Central Intelligence Agency
DCI	director of competitive intelligence
DGSE	Direction Générale de la Sécurité (France)
EAP	employee assistance programme
EBIT	earnings before interest and taxation
FBI	Federal Bureau of Investigation (US)
HUMINT	human source intelligence
IMINT	imagery intelligence
JETRO	Japan External Trade Organization
KIQ	Key Intelligence Question
KIT	Key Intelligence Topic
M&A	mergers and acquisitions
MASINT	measurement and signature intelligence
MBTI	Myers-Briggs Type Indicator
MITI	Ministry of International Trade and Industry (Japan)
OSINT	open source intelligence
RoE	return on equity
S&T	scientific and technical
SBU	strategic business unit
SCIP	Society of Competitive Intelligence Professionals
SDECE	Service de Documentation Extérieure et de Contreespionnage (France)
SEIB	senior executive intelligence briefing
SEWS	Strategic Early Warning System
SIGINT	signals intelligence
SVR	Russian Foreign Intelligence Service
TSCM	technical surveillance countermeasures

Doing the right thing vs doing the thing right

INTRODUCTION

Intelligence represents the 'flip side' of the strategy coin. As one former US Director of Central Intelligence reminds us, 'the first comprehensive intelligence organization in America's history' was the Office of *Strategic* Services (OSS), the Second World War predecessor of the Central Intelligence Agency (Colby, 1978). In order, therefore, to appreciate both the nature and application of intelligence in the corporate setting, it is necessary first to refresh our thinking about some of the principal notions of strategy and its implications for organizational performance.

So, just what is strategy? Is it a special way of thinking? Is it process? Does strategy represent first and foremost a firm's portfolio of future options? Or has strategy come to mean something more akin to 'revolution' in the so-called, and now partially discredited, 'New Economy'? Indeed, is the very notion of 'strategy' even relevant to companies, and to those who lead them, in a post-industrial era? And so what? In practice does strategy have anything to do with the realities of satisfying customers, building brands, clawing in yet one more point of market share, meeting next quarter's financial objectives or seizing the high ground from competitors in the markets of tomorrow? If it works, isn't it, then, anyway strategic? Take your pick. From the endless torrent of books and papers on the subject which swamp our bookshelves, one could be forgiven for selecting any one or 'all of the above'. And ultimately, we ask, does strategy – or what one scholar terms 'strategic supremacy'® (d'Aveni, 2001) – even matter?

Strategy, as we know, has always mattered in warfare. And it certainly matters in the national security arena. Here we argue that strategy matters no less in today's hypercompetitive business environment, where few companies remain isolated for long from the rapidly changing dynamics of industry transformation and the disequilibrium that often results. Indeed, it is within this context that strategy, underpinned by intelligence, serves as the mechanism that 'offers a clear direction to allow managers to discern important decisions and focus on them in the midst of many distractions' (Porter, 2000). As such, strategy represents 'the power not only to stake out your own turf on [your industry's playing] field, but also to influence the positioning and maneuvering of your rivals' (d'Aveni, 2001). It embodies the firm's explicit 'plans to attain outcomes consistent with the organization's missions and goals' (Wright et al., 1992). Or, as the consulting firm McKinsey & Company put it, strategy involves the 'integrated set of activities designed to create a sustainable advantage over competitors' (Coyne, 2000). Strategy, in short, is the firm's theory about how to achieve and sustain competitive advantage. But gaining competitive advantage without a clear understanding of what your company is likely to be up against on its chosen playing fields – without credible intelligence about competitor intent and strategies – is, at best, luck and, at worst, a one-way ticket to failure.

Unfortunately, and to the great cost of many tens of thousands of employees and other stakeholders worldwide, many of our corporate leaders have failed to recognize that strategic competence and success cannot in fact exist without equal and parallel competencies in the twin disciplines of intelligence – in particular strategic intelligence – and counterintelligence. While intelligence is by no means a panacea for competitive success, to steer a major enterprise forward in an intelligence vacuum is pure folly – it is as rational an act as driving a car in total darkness without headlamps. Thus, the central theme of this briefing is that strategy without intelligence isn't strategy, it's guessing. Our objective is to address the central roles that intelligence and counterintelligence play in organizational strategy and policy-making, and to explain why, in what many of us now call an 'information age', executives need to understand and leverage intelligence in very much the same way that their counterparts do in government and the military.

To be effective, executives must be skilful in crafting strategy at all levels – corporate, business and functional. Equally, as the principal users, or 'consumers', of intelligence, they bear a responsibility for knowing what intelligence is, where it adds value to their day-to-day challenges and decision-making responsibilities, what it can, and cannot, deliver, something about how it is acquired and interpreted, and how it works or can be made to work for them. The aim of this chapter is to introduce the concept of strategic intelligence and its relevance to the real challenges of a 'globalized' business world, a world where there are more of those ready to grab a slice of the economic pie than that pie can readily feed.

SOME BACKGROUND

Any discussion regarding intelligence and its role in business strategy and the strategy process of the firm rests on three basic propositions advanced by Professor Michael Porter at Harvard Business School:

1. *The determinants of company performance are two-fold: (1) operational effectiveness and (2) strategic positioning.* While improving operational effectiveness or 'doing the thing right' may lead to absolute – rather than relative – organizational improvement, at the same time it tends to lead to competitive convergence. If, say, all competitors in an industry were to achieve perfect efficiency in 'best practices', no single player or set of players could be said to possess operations-based advantage. All players are running the same race in essentially the same way. Strategic positioning or 'doing the right thing', on the other hand, involves running a different race – or, as Porter notes, creating a unique and sustainable competitive position. Thus the essence of competitive advantage is rooted in the notion of differentiation. But differentiation is not simply a function of product or service differentiation. Differentiation, we maintain, and therefore

the contest between basic business models has a far greater impact on competitive performance today than any other aspect of business rivalry.

2. *The sources of long-term industry profitability can be defined in terms of the so-called 'five forces' model of industry dynamics.* This model serves as the cornerstone of industry and competitive analysis, and continues to provide the single most effective high-level strategic framework available for interpreting and explaining the external environment, the principal focus of intelligence operations. Figure 1.1 shows the 'five forces' model with two additional forces: (1) complementary products and services, or 'complementors', and (2) government policy. A company is a complementor if customers value your product more when they have the other company's product than whey they have your product alone (e.g. personal computers and Windows® operating systems; DVD players and DVDs; mobile phones and network services). Consider this question: how deep an understanding do you possess of your competitors' network of relationships with complementors, with major suppliers and with government departments and agencies?

Fig. 1.1 Porter's 'five forces' model

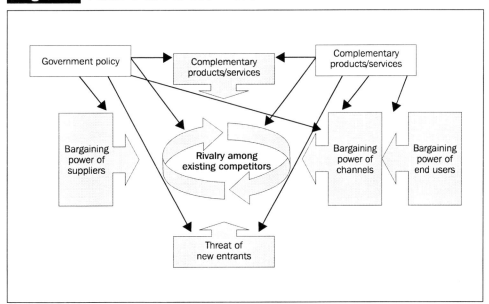

3. *'Value chain' activities – the primary and support activities of the firm – must be configured to match the strategy of the organization, not the other way around.* Dell Computer, for example, has outperformed major rivals such as Compaq, Hewlett-Packard (H-P) and IBM in the PC domain for years; its 'value chain' is configured differently to match the company's different business model and strategy, not the other way around. When, in the mid to late 1990s, for example, H-P's PC division were struggling with the problem of how to successfully compete against Dell, they were unwilling to seriously

consider the option of abandoning their existing channels of distribution for a direct sales model. Dell's costs were some 20 per cent less than H-P's, with products of apparently equal or similar standard, but H-P's 'marriage' to their traditional channel marketing strategies – a critical 'business blindspot', so to speak – prevented the company from capturing the market share and above average returns that otherwise could have been theirs to take.

Consider, too, the case of the firm Inditex based in Corunna (Spain) and its nearly 500 Zara stores worldwide. In the highly volatile retail fashion sector, Inditex[1] delivered 26 per cent return on equity (RoE) and a 10½ per cent net return on sales in 2001, a year when other clothing chains watched their sales and profits collapse. The company's business model is different. It is not based on lower costs, as is so often the case in an industry that increasingly farms out production to Third World manufacturers. Instead, Zara's success is based on a strategy which defines competitive advantage in terms of time to market, coupled with a unique value chain designed to match their strategy. These and similar examples raise the following questions for managers. How complete an understanding of your competitors' business models do you have, and their relative strengths and weaknesses versus your own? To what extent is your understanding of the way your competitors do, and plan to do, business based on recent, evidence-based intelligence, rather than outdated sets of assumptions?

Unfortunately, managers in most companies with whom we've worked appear to be perfectly content with 'getting on with the real business at hand', even as their companies attempt to weather today's increasingly fierce and unpredictable business and geopolitical storms. In the main, they do what they get paid to do rather than think more broadly – more strategically – about rivals and other external forces banging at the walls of their cozy corporate castles. They seek refuge in the myth that the strategies they and their planning staffs have so carefully crafted, sometimes with the aid of top consultancies, are 'as good as we're going to get' and represent 'the way the world really works'. The result: a growing number of companies, top names as well as rising stars – or would 'black holes' be more accurate? – just don't get it right. Major merger and acquisition deals fail – AOL/Time Warner, France Telecom/Orange, Marconi/Fore Systems, Vivendi/Seagram, WorldCom/MCI to name but a few – and, with increasing frequency, promises of more growth and higher returns in the future fail to materialize. So where, we ask, were the 'early warning' bells that should have sounded the alarm of impending threats? At what stage in the due diligence process, for example, were these companies' intelligence teams instructed to deliver estimates to management of the strategic implications and likely outcomes of impending 'marriages'? And where, in so many of these same cases, we ask, was the intelligence that could well have alerted management to the apparently hidden obstacles ahead, and provided better insight into unfolding competitor plans and other developments? One cannot help but wonder how different the fortunes of companies such as Enron, Swissair and WorldCom – companies whose corporate 'bubbles' have so spectacularly and unhappily burst – might have been had their leaders shifted strategies in time to match the changing realities – the changing realities that provide the very stuff of intelligence work.

It is our contention that developing a deep understanding of what strategy involves, how it is linked with innovation and how intelligence can help ensure that strategic decision-making and the strategy process of the company amount to something more than a rigorous exercise in guesswork or capital budgeting are determining factors in a company's future chances for success and survival.

Consider, specifically, the strategic missteps of firms such as Swissair, BT and Webvan, all companies that are – or were! – generally regarded as competent in the execution of their respective business operations.

In October of 2001 the 70-year-old blue-chip carrier Swissair, crushed by debt, went into a spiral dive. The result was a bankruptcy that shook and embarrassed the whole of the Swiss nation. By the time of the airline's collapse, it had lost 80 per cent of its share value in less than a year. Its strategy pivoted around two themes: (1) buying stakes in small European regional carriers (plus a nearly 50 per cent interest in Sabena, the consistently loss-making Belgian airline, which itself crumpled into bankruptcy one month later), and (2) 'offering a superior product, improvement and refinement of [its] passenger services'. Substituting expensive acquisition games for strategic innovation did little more than accelerate the dilution of Swissair's brand value, and improving operational effectiveness may have helped meet passenger expectations but ultimately had little impact on changing the airline's relative industry position and profitability. Finally, intelligence at Swissair was something occasionally assigned to the marketing research staff by executives who, from time to time, would elect to have a look at competitors' existing operations and new product plans; not terribly helpful when the real aim should have been to out-think, outmanoeuvre and outperform adversaries. Unfortunately, Swissair's top management was rather less interested in using intelligence to help reassess and reconstruct the airline's flawed business model, than they were in benchmarking themselves against traditional industry operational practices.

Another example of a company that, if it once knew where it was going, clearly lost its way is BT. BT evolved into a corporate dinosaur in an industry characterized by unparalleled upside opportunities. It lost over £1bn for the financial year 2001 on a turnover of some £20½bn, and saw its market capitalization decline from more than £65bn in 1999 to about half that amount in 2001. BT, one might reasonably have expected, would have possessed well-honed strategies meticulously developed by experienced teams of executives and planners over time. Apparently not. Or if it did, the question becomes: to what extent was the strategic focus at BT on itself rather than its external environment and the future plans and strategies of its rivals? Not until its share price had plummeted from £13.50 to £3 in late 2001 did the company announce that its then chief executive, Peter Bonfield, would be stepping down. Perhaps players such as Orange and the ubiquitous Vodafone, both comparatively new and successful entrants in telecommunications, concentrated rather more on understanding the world outside the boardrooms of their own companies than the 'restructuring'-oriented top management at BT. Again, while intelligence functions have for some time existed at various levels in the BT empire, it would appear that whatever strategic analysis this may have revealed about the organization's missteps was not disseminated to, or worse not heeded by, the company's key decision-makers. Senior executives, CEOs included, who are prepared to modify their vision, strategy, or policies on the strength of changing truths remain a rare species in the management kingdom.

Webvan, the Silicon Valley-based home delivery company, took only 18 months to go from a bold and exciting strategy based on ultimately fulfilling every local delivery need – from groceries to dry cleaning to video rentals – to filing for Chapter 11 bankruptcy protection in July 2001. Just days prior to its collapse, Webvan's share price had imploded from a high of $30 in November 1999 to close at 6¢ – hardly a recipe for increasing shareholder returns. Webvan's strategy was to use the Internet in combination with an efficient distribution system to do the thing 'more right' than established supermarkets and other retailers. Good try, and fun while it lasted, but did Webvan believe that industry incumbents would roll over and play dead while it started to eat their lunch? Customer focus is essential, but seldom is only one company focusing on the same customers. The question is: how much weight did Webvan's management attach to ongoing intelligence about the fiercely competitive environment into which they so enthusiastically entered, rather than to their almost religious belief in the destiny they imagined? To what extent did Webvan's management probe the strengths, vulnerabilities, ambitions and likely responses to their moves by the incumbent retailers whose market share they sought to erode?

Now a few more hard questions to ask yourself: is our business concept – our core strategy, the means by which we leverage our strategic resources, our customer interface, our external networks – one which is 'so unlike what has come before that traditional competitors [will be] left scrambling' (Hamel, 2000)? Is our thinking about strategy grounded in a rigorous analysis of the industry, with a clear focus on critical uncertainties? Or does the prevailing conventional 'wisdom' of your company run something like this: 'Competitors? Sure we've got competitors, but we focus on customers, on technology, and on sound product development. As long as customers are satisfied competition will take care of itself.' Motorola once led the way in mobile telecommunications. Ericsson, too, sought, and for several years shared, a leadership position in mobile handsets and infrastructure. Both companies, however, despite solid market experience, strong technology foundations and well-schooled managers have given way to the Finnish firm Nokia, once a manufacturer of tyres and other commodity products. Nokia out-designed, out-innovated, and outmaneuvered the once mighty Motorola as well as its powerful neighbour Ericsson to claim first place in the race to the wireless future. By July 2002 the market capitalization of Nokia was 40 per cent greater than that of Motorola and Ericsson combined.

Does this seem familiar? Winning strategic performance – performance which translates into consistently exceptional results – can only be determined with the benefit of hindsight when boards of directors, the investment community and the *Financial Times* finally hold up their scorecards to announce last year's, or last quarter's results. It's a good thing chess players, military commanders and high-performance firms such as Microsoft, Nokia and 4Kids – the enormously successful licensors and merchandisers of Pokémon property – take a different view of the world, one where effective strategic performance means making the rules, making superior returns and generally making it happen.

STRATEGIC INTELLIGENCE: THE SINE QUA NON OF INTELLIGENT STRATEGY

The craft of intelligence today has evolved from what is commonly referred to as the 'second oldest profession'. According to the Bible (Numbers 13: 17) Moses sent 12 men 'to spy out the land of Canaan [to] see what the land is, and whether the people who dwell in it are strong or weak, whether there are few or many ... and whether the cities they dwell in are camps or strongholds, and whether the land is rich or poor.' Since then, of course, the 'craft of intelligence' has evolved considerably; indeed, one would be hard pressed to point to a government anywhere that does not possess an intelligence arm. Although modern foreign intelligence agencies represent a comparatively new phenomenon – Great Britain's Security Service (MI5) was founded in 1909 'with the task of collecting evidence of German planning for an invasion of the country'; France's Service de Documentation Extérieure et de Contreespionnage (SDECE), now Direction Générale de la Sécurité Extérieure (DGSE), was created in 1946; and America's Central Intelligence Agency (CIA) was born in 1947 – they share a common mandate: reduce uncertainty for policy-makers. The question which modern corporate executives must ask themselves is this: do their firms include intelligence staffs with a similar mandate? In other words, do CEOs and their management teams rely upon internal intelligence and counterintelligence departments to help them better know and understand the current realities of their external environments?

Strategic intelligence is designed to provide senior decision-makers 'with the "big picture" and long-range forecasts they need in order to plan for the future' (Berkowitz and Goodman, 1989). A recent study by the US Corporate Strategy Board (2000) summarized the activity of strategic intelligence as 'providing senior [corporate] decision makers with timely comprehensive information about the external environment for the explicit purpose of supporting strategy development.' The same study identified three distinct principals of strategic intelligence:

1. *Strategic intelligence should support senior decision makers in their capacity as strategists. Co-ordinators of strategic intelligence – [i.e. intelligence staff] – should tailor their research and analysis to the specific needs of participants in various strategy activities.*

2. *Strategic intelligence should monitor and analyse the issues that matter to strategy. As corporate strategy is concerned principally with the consequences of long-term, unexpected changes, strategic intelligence must track a broad array of indicators, with an emphasis on identifying changes that suggest large shifts in the future.*

3. *Strategic intelligence should be co-ordinated in the corporate centre. Corporate functions are best positioned to co-ordinate the analysis and interpretations of strategically relevant information that is critical to senior decision makers.*

A 'world-class' intelligence capability is geared to answering two types of questions for its 'consumers' or users:

1. *puzzles* – which can, in principle, be answered definitively if the necessary information is collected or is otherwise available;

2. *mysteries* – which 'cannot be answered with certainty even in principle [and may be] intertwined with what the [firm itself] does' (Treverton, 2001). Will a key alliance or channel partner remain loyal to us? Will a major player not already in one of our major product or technology domains decide to enter? Will, for example, the market for DVDs continue to grow rapidly, or will it collapse in the face of new and superior technology standards and sytems?

Market researchers and corporate librarians seldom piece together the puzzles or solve the frustrating mysteries that challenge management teams everywhere. It's not their job, and when they try they usually fail. These tasks, however, are the stock-in-trade of professional intelligence analysts.

As with any professional discipline, intelligence is a multifaceted thing. It involves activity. It involves knowledge. And it involves organization. It must not, however, be confused with market research, nor is it an 'information service' per se. Rather, strategic intelligence, together with its twin discipline, counterintelligence, represent the company's 'first line of defence' against threats to its operations, plans and strategic ambitions. As one former US Director of Central Intelligence put it: 'What clearly distinguishes information as suitable for intelligence exploitation is its relevance to US policy and interests' (Gates, 1987). How relevant to strategic decision-making is the information being 'pushed' up to your management today? Is it more closely aligned with risk management than it is with churning out colourful pie charts and graphs illustrating last year's market share and financial performance (or lack of it!)? Or is it simply more of the same? Moreover, does it always answer the 'so what' question? Does it, in other words, make a difference to what you decide or do?

Activity

Intelligence activity involves the user-driven process by which 'all-source' competitor, industry and market information important to organizational security – including competitor capabilities, intentions, performance and vulnerabilities – are *requested*, *collected*, *analysed* and *disseminated* to decision-makers. Intelligence, in effect, seeks access to information other parties are trying to deny. The intelligence process is best understood in terms of the 'intelligence cycle', the five-phase model used in the US and other national security environments:

1. *Planning and direction* – where decision-makers' intelligence needs are established.
2. *Collection* – the gathering of 'all-source' data and information from which finished intelligence is ultimately produced.
3. *Processing and exploitation* – the conversion of raw data – translation, for example – to forms suitable for the production of finished intelligence.
4. *Analysis and production* – the integration, evaluation and analysis of all available information and the preparation of various intelligence products.
5. *Dissemination* – the delivery of intelligence products to pre-defined 'consumers' or users.

The intelligence cycle and each of its phases are examined in Chapter 5.

Knowledge

Intelligence knowledge refers to the end-'products' of the intelligence process. Competitive intelligence products generally fall into one of five categories:

1. *Current* – timely indications of new developments likely to have a significant impact on ongoing executive decision-making.

2. *Estimative* – 'definitive', longer-range analyses and judgments regarding subjects of the greatest concern to top management, including geopolitical and geo-economic topics.

3. *Warning* – identification of developments – essentially threats – likely to have an immediate and adverse impact on organizational security, strategies or policy.

4. *Research* – concerned with medium- to longer-term competitor and other 'key player' issues.

5. *Scientific and technical* (S&T) – information and analysis on rivals' scientific and technical developments and capabilities.

We provide a detailed review of intelligence products, or deliverables, in Chapter 5.

Organization

Intelligence is also organization. It is the firm's formal intelligence system, or architecture. Some 20 years ago Porter noted that 'Compiling the data for a sophisticated competitor analysis probably requires more than just hard work … To be effective, there is the need for an organised mechanism – some sort of competitor intelligence *system* – to ensure that the process is efficient' (Porter, 1980). This observation is no less valid today. We discuss setting up a company's intelligence system in Chapter 7.

But what about benefits? What, managers ask, are the key 'bottom-line' benefits of intelligence, and specifically an intelligence system, to our organization? Consider the following list:

■ It helps avoid strategic surprise – the sudden realization that the company has been operating on the basis of erroneous threat perceptions – by providing 'early warning' of competitive threats. What indications are there that the competitor is about to make a particular move? an acquisition or alliance? a shift in strategic focus? a new technology breakthrough?

■ It helps executives challenge their own orthodoxies by shedding light on business blindspots, the 'incorrect assumptions about the competitive arena, typically about competitors, consumers, suppliers, or technology' that otherwise go untested, or unchallenged (Gilad, 1994).

■ It helps ensure that decisions and actions are based on foresight and insight rather than on 'gut feel' or 'industry experience' alone.

■ It provides managers with a unique source of unbiased news and analysis. No other function in firms fulfils this role. All other organizational units have a particular, often self-serving agenda to defend. Ask yourself: when was the last time I heard a marketing director, brand manager or manufacturing head deliver an unbiased report with no stake in the outcome of the decision? Once? Twice? Ever?

■ It reinforces a competitive culture in the organization by means of increased competitor awareness.

■ It helps promote an awareness of threats to the company's intellectual capital and the need for counterintelligence and countermeasures.

■ It helps minimize uncertainty. Despite the reams of information and analysis readily available to most decision-makers, they usually face substantive degrees of 'residual uncertainty'.

During the course of a consulting engagement with a European telecoms operator, we asked each member of the executive board who they turned to first for what they might define as 'intelligence'. Not one executive suggested that the company's intelligence team was the first 'port of call'. In virtually every instance it was 'friends' at investment banks or elsewhere that they turned to. While external 'networking' is unquestionably an important and natural social phenomenon in all industries, it is not a proxy for a professional intelligence organization dedicated to collecting, analysing and delivering evidence-based intelligence in response to users' needs.

Until and unless managers institutionalize intelligence as a core capability of the firm and fully integrate it into each and every phase of the strategy process of their businesses, their odds of gaining or sustaining competitive advantage will be no greater than those offered by the croupier at a blackjack table. And to deliberately engage in competitive warfare with an adversary who has already used intelligence to understand your capabilities and anticipate your moves and countermoves is tantamount to playing a business version of Russian roulette.

If intelligence is the servant of strategy, then does it not follow that executives, the 'masters' of strategy so to speak, should endeavour to understand the linkages and interdependence between the strategy process of the firms they run and the intelligence function that should underpin it? Intelligence is not a 'black box' of secret workings somehow divorced from the mainstream of strategic decision-making and action. It is, or must be, firmly embedded in the strategy process of the company, and it must be institutionalized if it is to add real actionable value to decision-making.

NOTE

1. Other stores in the Inditex group include Kiddy's Class, Pull & Bear, Massimo Dutti, Stradivarius and Oysho.

2

The strategy process

INTRODUCTION

As we have seen, intelligence is an essential ingredient of successful strategy. How then should intelligence be integrated into the strategy process? While every company employs its own particular process models – there is no 'one size fits all' approach – there are certain fundamental stages which form the basis of the generic model shown in Figure 2.1 and which can be adapted to most organizations. This chapter explains the role of intelligence in each component of the model.

Fig. 2.1 Generic strategy process model

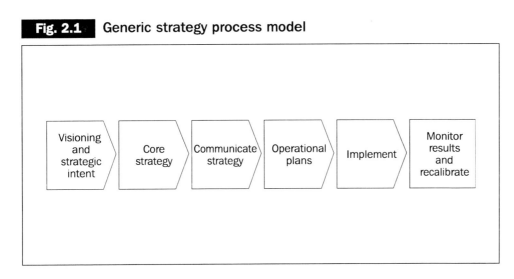

A strategy process serves as a framework or guideline. Its purpose is to ensure that companies, while remaining strategically adaptable, exercise some form of process discipline. The process cannot be too rigid, however, since it must accommodate the contribution and involvement of managers at all levels of the organization, corporate, divisional, business unit, functional and country/market. If, as some suggest, 'strategy is the organization', then the process by which it evolves, changes and is operationalized is arguably the company's most important process.

There are six main phases in the model. We will describe some of the key elements of each phase and explain the role intelligence plays in each.

VISIONING AND STRATEGIC INTENT

Although much has been written on the subject – naturally without any consensus on a single definition – vision does seem to possess the following characteristics:

■ It involves predicting the likely evolution of the external environment.

■ It involves seeking out discontinuities no one has identified in the industry.

- It means imagining the future the company wishes to create and shape. In 1992, Jorma Ollila, Nokia Corporation's chairman and CEO, summarized in four words his vision – ultimately adopted as the firm's strategic intent – of what Nokia ought to become by the year 2000: 'Focused, global, telecom-oriented, value-added'. This was at a time when telecommunications accounted for only about one-third of Nokia sales; by the autumn of 1993 the vision had been recast to: 'voice will go wireless'. And today, in Ollila's words: 'We want to be the company that brings the Internet to everybody's pocket.' Vision is not static.

- Vision is concerned with identifying unarticulated needs and unserved customer types.

- It provides descriptors for the key assumptions on which strategy development is ultimately based.

Intelligence has a critical, and especially challenging, role to play in the visioning phase of the strategy process. In essence, its job is one of performing a 'reality check'. Does the vision correspond to what is possible (if not probable)? Is the vision unique – are there other players who imagine a similar future and their roles in shaping it? What obstacles are adversaries capable of placing in the way of achieving the vision? What are the industry, geopolitical and geo-economic factors that might impede realization of the vision? Intelligence, in short, seeks to ensure that the firm 'has a better grasp of the future than its competitors do' (Porter, 2000).

Visionaries, predictably, are seldom objective enough to face strong challenges to their view of the future, and that is unlikely to change. Nevertheless, to ignore the hurdles that lie ahead in translating vision into action – indeed profitable action – is to fall prey to the trap that snared so many failed dotcoms, and as well as giants such as Bertelsmann, Vivendi Universal and AOL Time Warner. Fantasies, however compelling, should not be allowed to be confused with legitimate business dreams and innovation. The mess at Enron should certainly have taught us that.

A company's strategic intent is what should make it 'dangerous'. It flows from vision but is more precise. Hamel and Prahalad (1994) argue that strategic intent conveys a sense of direction, destiny and discovery. Strategic intent is the expression of the company's long-term aspiration for market dominance.

Nokia, for example, defines its strategic intent thus: 'to take a leading brand-recognised role in creating the Mobile Information Society by combining mobility and the Internet and by stimulating the creation of new services.' A company's strategic intent should represent the driving force behind all that it does. Its business ambitions, its strategies, its structures, its processes and the way it executes its plans in the marketplace should all flow from strategic intent in the high-performing, strategically managed firm.

INTELLIGENCE PROVIDES INSIGHT INTO COMPETITORS' STRATEGIC INTENT

Defining your own firm's vision and strategic intent is one thing. But what about the opposition? Key questions that senior executives should be asking their intelligence teams to investigate and assess at the start of the strategy process are:

- How do our competitors plan to 'compete for the future'?

- What is their vision, their strategic intent?

- How committed are they to achieving their declared strategic objectives? How, and where, might their objectives conflict with ours?

- What is the range of options open to us for dealing with unfolding new realities?

The alternative to discovering the answers to these questions amounts to little more than trusting the organization's fate to providence. Here the task of the intelligence team is not so much to report on competitors' capabilities – these, anyway, are generally well understood by management – but to determine rivals' core ambitions and intentions: intelligence that will only surface from information and opinions disclosed by a target firm's key decision-makers, and those who, whether inside or outside the company, influence or enjoy privileged access to strategic 'conversations'. This involves first and foremost a strong competence and tradition in human-source intelligence (HUMINT) collection and analysis. How, specifically, intelligence staff go about collecting, processing and analysing HUMINT and other information sources is the subject of Chapter 5.

CORE STRATEGY

A company's core strategy represents the centrepiece of its business model. It is, according to Hamel (2000), 'the essence of how the firm chooses to compete'. Its key elements include the company's business mission (what is the firm's overall objective?), the product/market scope of the organization (which customers will it seek to serve? in which geographies and with what products will it compete? where will it not compete?), and its basis for differentiation.

The core strategy of the firm involves defining such things as its value proposition, its 'big goals' and its performance objectives. It also involves defining its own distinctive value chain. Is the focus on performing different activities, or performing similar activities in different ways? Finally, a core strategy involves organizational plans and processes. Pekka Ala-Pietilä, the president of Nokia Corporation, explains it this way: 'Strategy = Structure = Implementation'.

Intelligence must at all times take the lead in arming management with analytically derived assessments of competitor business models, capabilities (resourcefulness, as well as resources!) and plans. If management do not possess a deep and continuously updated understanding of what the firm will actually be up against in the battles of the marketplace, including rivals' plans and intentions, how can there be any realistic expectation of winning the war? Swissair was surprised when British Airways first launched sleeper seats in first class in the late 1990s. The cost of that surprise was clearly measurable in terms of lost passenger miles from the industry's most profitable customer segment; where possible, long-haul first-class passengers switched to BA's more attractive, more highly added-value, offering at no additional cost.

Basic questions to ask your intelligence team about a rival's core strategy are as follows:

■ What is their business mission? Does their performance, and do their activities, match the mission? If not, how and why?

■ Where do they compete? In what product segments, and for which customers? How does this conflict, if at all, with our own company's ambitions?

■ How do they differentiate themselves and their offerings from us? From other competitors? What vulnerabilities can we exploit? Where do we not want to compete with them?

COMMUNICATE STRATEGY

The successful implementation of strategy requires that it is communicated throughout the organization, as well as to the investment community and other stakeholders. How otherwise can a company's workforce be expected to act with any degree of consistency, harmony and uniformity? Companies where not everyone is rowing in the same direction tend to find themselves stuck in the centre of their industry lake.

But there are dangers in the widespread disclosure of certain elements of detail. A pharmaceutical company's strategy may call for capturing the leading position in a particular therapeutic area, but it is certainly under no obligation to divulge the status of clinical trial development to the outside world in its race to be first to market. If a central aim of intelligence is to discover key aspects of rivals' strategies, then, conversely, there exists a need for a counterintelligence function to help manage the protection of one's own secrets and one's own competitive intelligence operations.

Corporate counterintelligence, the subject of Chapter 9, is concerned, in part, with protecting one's own competitive intelligence operations from disruption. In an industrial setting, it is also concerned with minimizing the 'loss' or disclosure of information likely to be of intelligence value to opponents.

Consider the following scenario. A large European manufacturer of packaged foods, as part of its strategy to grow its business substantially in Asia-Pacific, decides to launch one of its biggest selling premium brands in Malaysia and Singapore. This is intended to be the first phase in a much wider marketing effort throughout the region. Competition in this product segment is fierce, and seizing the dominant position relative to other European and American rivals rumoured to be planning similar initiatives is essential for success. Is it necessary, a counterintelligence officer might ask, to announce in the company's internal newsletter – complete with supporting photographs – that a senior brand manager and his evidently happy family are preparing for a new posting in Singapore when the product in question has not yet been launched in that market? What is the trade-off, in terms of strategically relevant information, between that which is gained by 'public' disclosure versus that which is lost? When a strategic initiative is unexpectedly 'shot down' as a result of a competitor's pre-emptive strike, it may prove instructive to ask: could painting a bull's eye on ourselves have had anything to do with it?

The principal role of counterintelligence in communicating strategy is, quite simply, to ensure that not too much detail is disclosed too early to too many. It is, after all, claimed that 'the devil is in the detail'. A well run company will ensure that every manager, indeed every employee, understands the 'grand strategy'. Equally, we caution, a well managed company does not hand the components of its operating plans on a silver platter to the wolves outside and say 'bon appétit'.

Key factors to consider:

■ Have we trained our staff to recognize, and assess the potential for, inadvertent disclosure of proprietary and other sensitive information in the ordinary course of external communications?

■ Does our approval process for external communications strike the right balance between getting the right 'messages' out and minimizing the risk of giving the information game away to circling rivals?

Key questions to ask your intelligence team regarding corporate communications:

■ What policies or procedures are in place that provide for the vetting of announcements, articles, papers, public presentations and the like by intelligence?

■ How much training in counter-elicitation have managers and staff in corporate communications, investor relations, marketing and other functions dealing with the 'outside world' received within the past year? Ever?

■ What are the procedures for handling external telephone calls? Do these procedures include centrally coordinated monitoring and analysis?

OPERATIONAL PLANS AND IMPLEMENTATION

Short-term planning concerns issues such as specific brand or product marketing and sales targets, and how they are to be achieved. Short-term plans are basically tactical in nature. In the pharmaceutical industry, for example, they will typically involve issues such sales force size and the marketing 'messages' for doctors and health authorities.

Managers with brand, product, country and various functional responsibilities are the principal internal customers of tactical intelligence. Their needs tend to be more immediate, and relatively short term regarding 'outlook'. Intelligence in support of day-to-day operations is important but clearly provides 'less bang for the buck' than strategic intelligence. A platoon commander ordered to take a position will certainly want to know the disposition and, if possible, intentions of enemy forces. A product manager can more effectively anticipate, or respond to, competitors' promotional campaigns if he or she has some advance warning of what these might involve. In both instances intelligence can play a determining role in who wins the battle, but the costs associated with gaining the intelligence need to be carefully weighed against the expected value. The aim should be to employ intelligence consistently in operations, thereby accumulating a series of measurable successes.

Ultimately, any given 'piece of intelligence' may support either a strategic or tactical problem. It depends on the context. In practice, corporate competitive intelligence (CI) staffs tend to deal with matters of strategic consequence – business portfolio and acquisitions, say – whereas CI teams at the business unit level are involved with both tactical and strategic issues.

The Senior Director of Intelligence at McGraw-Hill Group in the United States thinks of tactical versus strategic intelligence in four principal dimensions (Belkine, 2001):

1. *Time.* Subject to the size and nature of company activity, short-term intelligence problems (weeks or several months) tend to be tactical in nature.

2. *Resource allocation.* Where resources are contributed by one department or business unit only, the problem is more likely to be tactical in scope.

3. *Results.* If the intelligence affects a single business, department, or function, it can usually be regarded as tactical.

4. *Perception.* The higher the organizational level concerned with the intelligence topic, the more it would tend to have strategic implications.

TRACKING/MONITORING

Intelligence is often the lone voice in the corporate wilderness that raises the alarm when 'things aren't going as planned' or when the future isn't quite unfolding as we might have expected or wished. Many managers demonstrate a dangerous propensity for remaining wedded to that which they do and are committed to do. The strategy made sense. The planning was thorough. So, despite evidence to the contrary of changed and changing external circumstances, they continue with the mission at hand – very much like the captain of the *Titanic*, and often with similar results. One critical role of intelligence, both at the strategic and tactical level, is to alert management to new external realities that are having, or will likely soon have, an unhappy impact on the firm's agenda. Business is not a horse race – if it becomes obvious that we are going to lose the contest we must reassess the position and either do something differently or withdraw. In business, as in warfare, retreat is often the better part of valour.

Finally, one of the greatest errors made by managers is to assume that competitive intelligence is somehow a subset of marketing intelligence or research, and that the scope of its activities is, and should therefore be, limited to marketing support. We have argued, on the other hand, that intelligence has a critical role to play in each phase and in every element of the strategy process. Where intelligence is ignored or missing, so too are winning strategies. And when firms lose the strategic race too often, at best a few heads at the top start to roll, and at worst the lawyers and receivers are called in to preside over yet another corporate funeral.

3

Key intelligence topics

INTRODUCTION

An effective intelligence system is user or policy driven; it exists for one purpose: to meet the decision-making needs of its consumers. In order to accomplish this mission intelligence must consistently deliver 'product' that addresses the issues of both immediate and long-term concern to management. And whereas yesterday's 'intelligence systems were designed for monitoring relatively static' threats – often with the principle focus on competitor capabilities and resources – today's business managers now 'need new systems that can establish and maintain a closer more constant watch on smaller, fleeting targets' (Pappas and Simon, 2002), like biotechnology and generics firms in pharmaceuticals or Silicon Valley start-ups in the technology sector. The tough part is knowing where and how to focus the intelligence efforts. What are the topics with which management needs to be concerned? How do we identify and define the critical decision challenges and information gaps? Competitive intelligence professionals refer to these topics as 'key intelligence topics' (KITs). This term was originally coined by Jan Herring, a former National Intelligence Officer for the directorate of Science and Technology at the US Central Intelligence Agency and later the director of Motorola's intelligence programme, and from whom much of our own thinking on the subject is based.

The aim of this chapter is to make it clear how executives should think about their intelligence requirements, and decide what they really need and should expect from their intelligence staff.

How does one begin to think about specific intelligence requirements? How do managers and intelligence analysts drill down through the infinite plethora of information available to them to determine those things that are essential to know about the external environment in which the organization competes or plans to compete? At the highest level, as noted in Chapter 1, a company typically starts with the Porter model of the 'five forces' driving industry competition. While this framework has proven to be robust over time, most executives today hardly need be reminded that they constantly face the pressures associated with intensifying competitive rivalry, the threats of substitute products and services, the threat of new entrants into their industries and markets, and the shifting 'bargaining powers' of customers and suppliers alike. An appreciation of the environmental forces that affect company and industry performance is necessary, but it is only a beginning.

In order to define executives' intelligence needs it is necessary, first, to think in terms of priorities:

- What are those strategically relevant issues or topics 'where the outcome or resolution has a significant impact on the value of the firm' (Hussey and Jenster, 1999)? The focus of intelligence is very different from that of market research, and it is certainly not a proxy for the corporate library function.

■ How, in effect, do we identify and define the legitimate intelligence needs of management?

Intelligence serves to help management advance and defend the strategic interests of the firm. But since few, if any, companies are prepared to write a blank cheque for intelligence operations – and indeed there is no compelling reason why they should – intelligence cannot support the needs of all managers at all times. Intelligence resources, unsurprisingly, are limited; despite what many CI personnel would wish to believe, intelligence is not a bottomless well from which all in the company may drink without regard to financial limitations. Consider your own company's annual budget for intelligence operations and its relative size compared to, say, advertising. Developing and launching a new advertising campaign certainly seems to merit a higher priority in firms than gaining a firm grip on the realities of environmental threats.

THE PROCESS

The KIT process is the mechanism by which the firm's intelligence staff identify and prioritize the organization's intelligence requirements.

This involves translating the key decision-making needs of managers into topics and questions that can be operationalized for collection and analysis by the competitive intelligence unit. Executives do not and should not necessarily be expected to think in terms of 'intelligence requirements'; rather, their responsibility is to articulate their concerns and decision challenges to intelligence personnel as part of an ongoing dialogue with them. It is the job of the CI unit to analyse these concerns and challenges, then express and agree them with their internal customers as KITs and KIQs ('key intelligence questions').

KITs possess three distinguishing features:

1. They represent the careful development of a series of collection-based key intelligence questions, systematically developed from the interaction between intelligence staff and the intelligence 'owner' or consumer.

2. They are a statement regarding the implications of the topic for the company – the attempt to answer, in effect, the 'so what?' question: what's the analysis, what does this mean for the organization?

3. They are part of 'an ongoing, intelligence needs identification process', not a simple 'question and answer' activity (Herring, 2002).

Thus, KITs are used to:

■ guide and focus intelligence collection and organize and set priorities for analysis;

- provide 'critical inputs into the design and planning of the new [or existing] intelligence programme' of the company (Herring, 2002).

There are four categories of KITs, examined in detail below, which serve as the basic framework managers and intelligence analysts alike should use when defining their requirements:

1. decision topics;
2. key player topics;
3. warning topics;
4. counterintelligence topics.

DECISION TOPICS

Decision topics generally spring from current intelligence needs that arise in the various phases of the strategy process. They are characterized by an end-date – the intelligence deliverable is required within a certain pre-defined time (after which it has no intelligence value) – and can concern virtually any pending business decision or action. For example, topics might concern the development and implementation of strategic plans, capital expenditure likely to affect competitive positioning or issues related to joint ventures, acquisitions and divestitures. In pharmaceuticals, for example, a topic might be expressed as: 'What is the current status of a competitor's drug development programme for compound "X"?' Some examples of the KIQs likely to be associated with this topic are:

- What is the expected product launch date?
- What is the planned filing procedure in Europe for regulatory approval? Centralized? Mutual recognition?
- What are the indications?
- What about dosage?
- Is the company aiming for a 'premium price'?
- What about their marketing strategies?

KEY PLAYER TOPICS

Key player topics are concerned with the activities, capabilities, intentions and plans of industry rivals and others. A partial list might include alliance and joint-venture partners, competitors (existing and emerging), major customers and suppliers, and influential pressure groups (the nuclear energy industry, for example, would be well advised to monitor the objectives, plans and actions of the so-called 'Greens' in Germany and elsewhere).

Key player topics are designed to provide a greater understanding of the capabilities and intentions of targets and deeper insight into their current and future actions. A major research-based pharmaceutical company might be concerned with the following issues regarding a rival:

■ What is the competitor's approach to capturing 'physicians' loyalty'? To retaining patients on their treatments?

■ What are the competitor's 'culture' and style?

  – With whom do they collaborate (research labs, universities, etc.)?

  – Risk takers?

  – How aggressive in terms of drug development and marketing?

  – Management personality profiles (e.g. MBTI[1]®)?

  – How do they perceive us? Our strategies and tactics?

Of the four categories of KITs, topics regarding key players are arguably the least 'actionable'. They are, however, important. Typically, in any 'group of managers each [will] have a different mental model of [a] player and because of that, they tend to think and act differently concerning that player' (Herring, 1999). One purpose of key player topics is to enable managers to develop a common, evidence-based understanding of the critical issues regarding target players. This, in turn, facilitates more effective debate and thinking about future decisions and actions about competitors and others.

Consider the results shown below of one exercise by the international division of a European telecoms operator to identify an important KIT – in fact something of a hybrid between a decision and key player topic – and its significance. The concern was over a larger, American-based player who had recently moved into Europe.

KIT

What are competitor's capabilities and strategic intent regarding wholesale business in the 'heart of Europe'?

Company internal customers

■ Director (CEO)

■ VP Strategy & Acquisitions

■ VP Operations Consulting

Decision impact

- 'Wholesale market' investment strategy
- Board of directors review

Implications

- Defending the core business

KIQs

- How does competitor define its core business? What is the rationale for infrastructure development?
- How much do they deviate from this? And why?
- How does competitor view company?
- How does competitor plan to grow? What are the profit and market share objectives?
- What is the R&D direction? Why?
- Top management profiles:
  - Successes and failures
  - Are they 'known' players?
  - What is their image?
  - What are their real responsibilities?
- Profiles of competitor's partners:
  - Who are they?
  - Why are they partners? What are their agreements/licences?
- What are competitor's supplier relationships?
- Who are their customers?
- How does competitor recruit? From where?
- How important is middle management to competitor?

WARNING TOPICS

A 'strategic early warning system' (SEWS), as described in Chapter 4 of this briefing, represents the cornerstone of a firm's competitive intelligence programme. Warning topics are those topics which are routinely monitored or tracked against pre-determined indicators, with no fixed end-date. Warning topics often reflect executives' suspicions or 'fears', if not a little paranoia, and start from the presumption that there are no 'happy surprises' in business. A warning topic, therefore, is one way of dealing with the question: 'What would we do if we were them?' Or perhaps more to the point, a warning topic is designed to help us avoid having to ask the question raised by one group of authors after the terrorist attacks of 11 September 2001 in America: 'How did this happen?' (Hoge and Rose, 2001).

The three principal aims of an early warning topic are to:

1. identify current and future threats, including 'disruptive' changes in the industry, in government and in technology;

2. avoid strategic surprise, especially competitor initiatives;

3. spot new business opportunities.

A set of early warning topics for a company in the laundry products business might look like this:

Acquisitions, alliances and divestitures
Are our competitors planning to:

- acquire companies that could improve their most important technology platforms, or market share position?

- divest or cancel product lines?

- forge alliances or joint ventures with firms likely to give them a unique advantage in laundry products?

Product initiatives
What about:

- new product development?

- intentions or plans to launch or extend brands/products?

- new packaging and delivery systems?

Technology
What developments are underway regarding product, production and packaging technologies?

Key customers and distribution systems
Any changes in competitors' plans, activities or relationships with our firm's key customers? Supply agreements, exclusive marketing agreements, and joint e-commerce initiatives are of particular interest.

> *Retail environment*
> Are competitors planning to introduce any radical new approaches to in-store selling?

COUNTERINTELLIGENCE TOPICS

While the subject of counterintelligence is covered at some length in Chapter 9 of this briefing, it is essential that such topics are not overlooked or ignored as an essential component of the KIT process. Counterintelligence topics deal with at least four sets of important questions regarding the protection of a company's knowledge assets:

1. What must our firm protect?
2. What are our competitors (or foreign government agencies) trying to discover about us? And why?
3. How are they trying to do it?
4. What can we do, and what are we doing, to reduce their chances of getting it? What legitimate denial and deception tactics might we employ to safeguard our proprietary information?

Despite an overwhelming set of evidence that should frighten any reasonable manager into taking counterintelligence seriously (see, for example, ASIS/PwC LLP, 1999), it is our experience that, in Europe at any rate, most managers cannot answer the first two questions. The result is that they are not equipped to provide an appropriate answer to the third and fourth questions. Ask any modern manager what his company's most valuable assets are and the response will almost certainly be 'our people', or more accurately the knowledge – especially proprietary knowledge – and competencies of the employees who make up the company. Knowing who is trying to steal or otherwise gain access to the most valuable elements of that knowledge and how they are trying to do it represents a fundamental responsibility of any organization. Counterintelligence topics will, at times, represent the most critical issues for intelligence focus, such as when merger or acquisition negotiations are underway. After all, allowing information that lies at the very heart of a firm's competitive advantage to 'walk', unhindered, 'out the door' into the hands of rivals is hardly the stuff of effective risk management.

In practice, the most challenging aspect of defining KITs involves ongoing interaction between executives and CI staff. This is partly a function of good time management – are executives really too busy to turn their attention to protecting the future of the organization? But it is also related to the social – rather than technical – processes associated with the human dynamics between intelligence and management. If intelligence is to deliver useful, relevant results, it must enjoy direct access to decision-makers. This means regular meetings between intelligence managers and analysts and their internal customers. This means executives cooperating with intelligence in semi-formal interview sessions. And this means feedback: intelligence cannot add, or continuously upgrade, its 'value added' to organizational decision-making if it does not know how its product is used and perceived by managers. Although well established CI departments do, over time, develop a competence in anticipating intelligence requirements, their focus can very soon become 'academic' if not subject to the rigour that stems from 'being close to the customer'.

As Herring (1999) puts it:

For management, their stated needs for intelligence – by whatever process – provides them with actionable access to CI resources throughout the company. For the intelligence professional, well-defined intelligence needs are the prescription for planning and carrying out the right intelligence operations and producing appropriate intelligence products.

In intelligence, as with most business endeavours, there is no substitute for understanding what is needed, who needs it and why, and when it is needed by. The 'Key Intelligence Topics Survey Form' (*see* Figure 3.1) is designed to be used as part of an intelligence audit to help determine individual executives' KITs. This, of course, is only the first step in the process. Before starting any intelligence activity, company intelligence staff 'must be sure that [they] have the KIT issues right and the executive understands what will be done and can be expected as far as the final results' (Herring, 2002), which, in turn, involves ongoing dialogue between managers and intelligence.

Trying to make sense of the avalanche of random data and information which overwhelm us all today is an impossible challenge. But identifying management's real intelligence needs and priorities, and then fulfilling these requirements within the context of a focused, systematic intelligence gathering and analysis process is not, and represents the value and very purpose of the KIT framework.

NOTE

1. MBTI is the acronym for Myers-Briggs Type Indicator, a psychological instrument used to help predict behaviour. Its application in the competitive intelligence domain involves carrying out remote psychological assessments of the leaders of 'target' firms.

Fig. 3.1   Key Intelligence Topics survey form

KITs SURVEY

Purpose

To identify your Competitive Intelligence (CI) needs

To understand how you would use intelligence

To obtain your ideas and suggestions regarding how the intelligence function, or system, can best be developed by the company

I. Intelligence Needs

A. *Decision-making (your area of responsibility)*

■ Planned/future

■ Past examples

■ Sources of external information

- written inputs

- experts

- personal network

■ Decision-making process:

- within business unit/division

- for the company

■ Suggestions to improve the quality of external information needed to make decisions

B. *Early warning intelligence*

■ Examples of past surprises

■ Concerns about the:

- company

- business

- industry

- other

■ Subjects about which you believe the company needs to be well informed but at present is not

C. *Competitors*

■ Which competitors are you most concerned about?

■ What types of information intelligence do you need?

■ What uses do you make of competitor intelligence?

continued

D. Awareness

- Topics that you must regularly follow to do your job well

- External issues that have an impact on your business strategies and operations (e.g. country risk, terrorist threats, regulatory)

II. Intelligence Uses

- What uses do you expect to make of intelligence (e.g. market research, product and/or technology development, strategic planning, sales)?

- Who in your organization do you expect to be regular users of intelligence?

- What types of intelligence 'products' would you like to see (e.g. field reports, intelligence briefings, assessments, long-range estimates, research reports, warning alerts)?

III. Intelligence Capabilities

- Experience/familiarity with intelligence

- What types of intelligence/information do you receive at present?

- What intelligence capabilities does your business unit/division presently possess?

- What intelligence capabilities does your business unit/division need?

- Will your business unit/division be able to conduct intelligence operations to help other units/divisions? Any barriers?

- In your view, how should your company's intelligence system be organized?

IV. Comments, Ideas, Suggestions

- Today

- Afterthoughts (anytime)

4

Early warning

There should be no doubt in anybody's mind [that Saddam Hussein] is thumbing his nose at the world, that he ... is trouble in his neighbourhood, that he desires weapons of mass destruction. I will use all the latest intelligence to make informed decisions about how best to keep the world at peace ...

... America needs to know, I'll be making up my mind based upon the latest intelligence ... how best to protect our own country plus our friends and allies.

President George Bush, August 2002

INTRODUCTION

A 'strategic early warning system' (SEWS) lies at the very heart of a firm's competitive intelligence programme. It involves 'the earliest possible identification of dynamic or idiosyncratic features of a situation which may affect company interests' (Sawka and Fiora, 1997). It is the mechanism by which firms anticipate, detect and where possible prevent, or at least mitigate, strategic surprise. The purpose of early warning, in short, is to better prepare managers for possible crises and competitive conflicts and at times help prevent them.

Early warning of impending competitor moves represents one of the most difficult missions of the firm's intelligence department, because in business, as in war, 'surprise is almost always unavoidable ... despite all efforts to the contrary' (Handel, 1989). Whereas the company almost always knows the capabilities and resources of existing rivals, managers frequently are ill informed about future competitor intent or potential competitive threats posed by new industry and market entrants. Indications regarding intent are often ambiguous, and are unlikely to be deciphered in the absence of constant monitoring and analysis. Warning is, of course, also time sensitive – a warning alert must be disseminated to decision-makers in sufficient time to take action. Indeed, in practice early warning of competitive threats and opportunities is often the only thing that stands between competitive success and organizational surprise. Surprise acts as an important force multiplier in warfare, and, similarly, represents one of the key elements for success on the battlefields of today's marketplaces. While throwing up one's hands in bewilderment when a competitor makes an unexpected move may represent a natural human reaction, it certainly contributes little to shoring up the firm's strategic deficiencies or intelligence gaps. No major initiative takes place without some indication that 'something is cooking'. The trick, of course, is in identifying the indicators early enough to determine what they mean and what needs to be done to pre-empt or respond to the impending event.

Ideally, a warning, or sometimes series of warnings, is issued early enough to allow decision-makers to initiate countermeasures and thereby prevent the warning threat from actually materializing. But the reality is often very different, for example: a competitor's unexpected product launch or entry into a new (and previously 'safe') segment or territory; the surprise announcement of an alliance, acquisition or merger between competitors; the collapse of a major customer or supplier; or the introduction 'overnight' of commercially penal laws or regulations in a key overseas market.

NO HAPPY SURPRISES

In business, as in warfare, there are no happy surprises. Thus, 'few functions of intelligence are as important to [companies] as accurate forecasting, or warning, of events which could adversely affect' the interests or security of the organization (Grabo, 1987). And despite the excuses which regularly feature in the introduction to annual reports of companies that have underperformed, there are few events which 'erupt so suddenly that there are no hints of impending trouble well before the situation becomes acute' (Grabo, 1987).

The so-called warning problem is illustrated in the indications and warning model shown in Figure 4.1. The model attempts to explain that the further away in time one is from an event the greater the flexibility of the decision-maker. Conversely, the greater the time interval to the event the less certain one is of information or of the validity of information concerning the event. Warning intelligence, therefore, seeks to provide clearly discernible and actionable warnings about impending threats or opportunities as early as possible before the 'event' in order to boost decision-maker flexibility.

Fig. 4.1 Indications and warning model

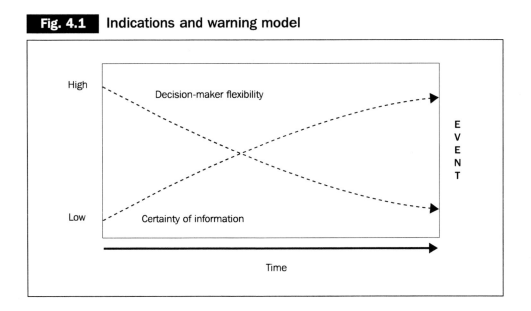

There are five central principles of early warning:

1. It is concerned primarily with the company's strategic interests, essentially future events likely to have a significant – and usually adverse – impact on those interests. Useful warning intelligence is something that makes a difference to decision-making. Conversely, tactical warning, which is very short term, seldom permits decision-makers sufficient time to consider and plan an effective response.

2. The focus is on the monitoring of pre-defined indicators of an approaching change in 'current state'. For example, if the CEO or, say, the director of mergers and acquisitions of a rival firm is discovered to have made a series of visits to the headquarters city of another competitor in a relatively short space of time, does this indicate that merger or acquisition negotiations are underway? Perhaps. Perhaps not. An indicator, by definition, signals the possibility, and sometimes probability, of a likely future event taking place.

3. While no intelligence analyst wishes to gain a reputation for 'crying wolf', overcoming analysts' hesitancy to 'sound the alarm' when an indicator is detected remains one of the toughest challenges in the intelligence environment. Analysts are sometimes reluctant to issue warnings unless they are satisfied, almost beyond doubt, that 'something is up'. As Andy Grove, co-founder and now Chairman of the Board of Intel, once observed, 'only the paranoid survive'.

   Consider the ill-fated bombing of the Chinese embassy in Belgrade on 7 May 1999 by a US B2 aircraft. According to US officials, a mid-level analyst, who was temporarily assigned to the Central Intelligence Agency, had some familiarity with the target building – the Yugoslav Federal Directorate for Supply and Procurement – and questioned whether intelligence officials developing target lists had the correct address. The analyst, officials claimed at the time, 'had no hint or notion that it was the Chinese Embassy. He just thought the headquarters building was some distance from the building selected.' On at least two occasions, the analyst raised his concerns that the building was not a military facility but did not insist that these concerns be conveyed to more senior officials. The result: one Chinese journalist killed, twenty others injured, and an embarrassing and costly international 'incident'.

4. Warning involves 'all-source' collection and analysis, that is the monitoring and interpretation of data and information – for the most part against pre-defined indicators – from both 'open' (OSINT) and human (HUMINT) sources. Warning intelligence in particular requires centralized direction and management. And because of the comparatively short 'shelf life' of any intelligence warning, companies must have mechanisms in place to ensure the efficient and rapid dissemination of warning intelligence to management.

5. Warning indications are often based on an assessment of capabilities only, with intent implied. This is dangerous. While it is a comparatively simple matter to quantify, say, the human, financial and other material resources of an organisation – and therefore their operational potential – it quite another matter to develop an actionable understanding of their thinking and often changing intentions. The central question facing the Kennedy administration during the so-called 'Cuban missile crisis' of October 1962 serves to illustrate the importance of knowing the opposition's intent: was the USSR's 'decision to put [offensive nuclear] missiles secretly in Cuba a new departure in Soviet policy indicative of a readiness to increase the level of risk in US–Soviet relations?' (Matthias, 2001). In the business arena, does a competitor's decision to acquire a leading firm in an entirely new technology domain signal a readiness, or strategy, to develop a new area of business?

ELEMENTS, OBJECTIVES AND PROCESSES

There are four critical elements in an intelligence warning 'product':

1. Information about the actor(s) involved: who are they? what do we know about them?

2. Nature of the threat or opportunity: what indications are pointing to what potential threat?

3. Probability of occurrence: terms such as 'could', 'likely', 'might', 'possibly', 'probably', 'we believe' or 'we do not believe' are typically used by analysts when articulating their judgment of probability. Unfortunately, each of these expressions is interpreted differently by different managers and is therefore often meaningless. It is the evidence supporting the judgment that matters, as well as the significance of the intelligence itself. Terrorist actions such as those that took place in America on 11 September 2001 may once have been considered improbable, but this should not have been allowed to diminish their significance in the event they were to – as indeed they did – occur. There is no room in intelligence reporting for the CYA syndrome.

4. Timing: when could it, or will it, happen? A week from now? Within the next quarter?

The objectives of early warning are therefore simply expressed:

1. Where possible, avoid a 'crisis' situation.

2. If (1) fails, manage the crisis to enable the achievement of strategic objectives.

3. If (2) fails, undertake pre-emptive action or countermeasures to mitigate or avoid a prolonged crisis.

4. If (3) fails, end the crisis on terms as favourable to the organization's interests as possible.

The responsibility of the company's competitive intelligence unit is to manage SEWS against three criteria:

1. Timing – when to warn.

2. Selectivity – what to warn.

3. Style – how to warn.

Figure 4.2 – adapted from a model originally developed by the US consulting firm the Futures Group – portrays the process involved in building a warning framework.

Fig. 4.2   Building a warning framework

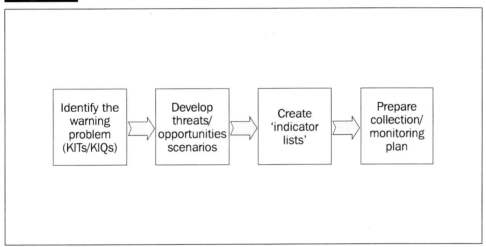

In this framework, the first step involves identifying warning KITs and KIQs (the subject of Chapter 3). Second, company executives, together with CI staff, need to develop plausible scenarios – not predictions – of likely competitive threats (or conflicts) and opportunities. Here one would wish to consider not only historical precedents, but potential risks and opportunities. In the third phase, the intelligence team will wish to draw up a list of indicators for each competitive situation – those events or actions that suggest a possible change in current state. For example, what are those 'signals' that might suggest a rival's change in technology direction, a new positioning strategy or potential merger or acquisition? In the fourth phase of the process the CI unit prepares a collection plan for monitoring or tracking the indicators. Ultimately, in their continuous efforts to separate the 'signals from the noise', competitive intelligence analysts need always to ask:

1. Is the perceived move unambiguous? Is the competitor's purpose clear?

2. Does it appear necessary, rather than optional, that we prepare, say, for the competitor's 'attack' or initiative?

IT'S UP TO MANAGEMENT

Early warning, of course, is as much a question of policy-making as it is one of intelligence. Few executives 'act, strategize, or decide outside the limits of the known world', the industry and market environments with which they have become all too comfortably familiar (Baumard, 1994). It was not until Dell Computer – who do not, after all, develop, make or sell anything new in the way of PCs or servers – began to seize market share from the industry incumbents that managers at companies such as Compaq, Hewlett-Packard and IBM began to reassess their own business concepts and strategies. But it was too little too late. By early 2002 Dell Computer had captured the number one worldwide market share position in terms of PC shipments. This was accomplished by operationalizing a direct sales business model that the leading industry players had simply ignored.

Unfortunately the history of business is littered with examples of decision-makers failing to respond, or respond adequately, to warning. Warning and response 'despite their close relationship, are not linked to each other either directly or inextricably'. A warning may not be perceived as sufficiently accurate or believable by decision-makers, and at times it may indicate the possibility of the 'unthinkable'. And at times decision-makers may simply fail to act on intelligence warning. The administration of President Johnson chose to ignore explicit intelligence warnings pointing to what resulted in the widespread communist uprisings in South Vietnam in January 1968 – the so-called Tet offensive. In this instance American confidence in its national leadership, as well as the country's will to prosecute the war, was shattered. And the costs? The US spent seven more years engaged in a conflict it could not win, sacrificing tens of thousands of lives and any sense of national unity or purpose in the process. Companies who refuse to remain alert to changing external forces likely to have an impact on their businesses do not suffer human casualties in quite the same way, but the profound financial, social and psychological consequences of failure for employees, shareholders and their communities are hardly the stuff of fairytales with happy endings.

Early warning, we have argued, is principally concerned with alerting executives to an impending event in order to prevent or minimize the effects of such an event. It is a special form of risk assessment, one where wrong assumptions or incorrect estimates about the potential impact of threats can easily lead to flawed decisions. And thus it must be managed with great sensitivity and professionalism. But the benefits of an effective SEWS, including preparedness, prevention and mitigation – factors which all too often are missing from the strategic behaviour of firms – means that it is too important a function to be ignored or overlooked by the corporate powers that be.

Intelligence as activity: the process

INTRODUCTION

In Chapter 1 we referred to the intelligence cycle and its five interdependent steps or phases. As in most systems, each phase is as essential as the others, and each phase adds value. While in practice the process is multi-directional, multi-dimensional and iterative, it is better understood when explained as a linear flow model (*see* Figure 5.1). We have found that, if managers are to realize the full potential of intelligence, some degree of transparency is helpful in understanding what can and cannot be expected from it. In the following sections of this chapter we discuss each phase in turn.

Fig. 5.1 Intelligence process

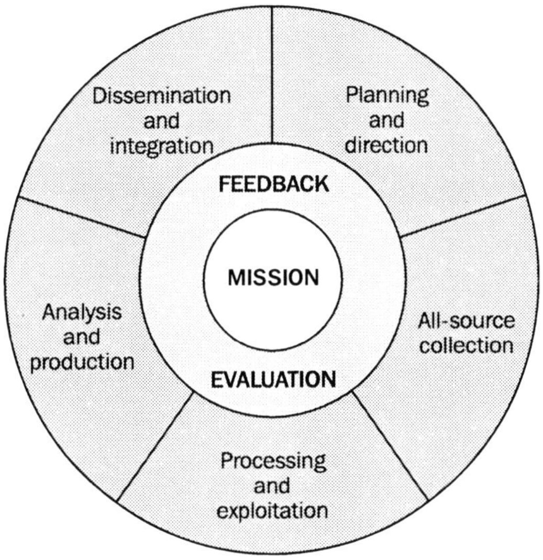

PLANNING AND DIRECTION

The intelligence process begins when managers express their needs for crucial information – in particular information and analysis not otherwise available from conventional sources – to help them accomplish their missions. A useful starting point for defining intelligence needs is to think in terms of six basic questions:

1. Who?

2. What?

3. Where?

4. When?

5. Why?

6. How?

Consider for a moment the intelligence requirements of a manufacturer of heavy-duty gas turbines that we shall call EuroPower. Their intelligence needs regarding a major competitor, who we will refer to as CanGen, might well concern topics involving costs and prices, strategy, manufacturing capacity and technology. For example:

- What do CanGen propose to spend on R&D in the area of gas turbine technology (absolute and relative to revenues) during the next five years? What was the spending over the past five years?

- What is the actual blade lifetime for the turbine blades of CanGen's X1 and X2 gas turbine models?

- How have CanGen been able to triple production from 2000 to 2002? To what extent do they use agile manufacturing? What role did shorter cycle times play in the significant expansion of their production capacity? What are their current cycle times, and what are their goals for the future in this respect?

- When and where (which customer?) do they plan to introduce their new Super-X3 gas turbine system? Why have they chosen the new, apparently more expensive, technology platform for the Super-X3?

These needs are then reformulated by the intelligence group into key intelligence topics, as discussed in Chapter 3.

Intelligence needs are used to guide collection activities and, ultimately, the production of appropriate and timely intelligence products. After all, it is in the planning phase where intelligence staff and intelligence users establish and agree the users' core concerns and associated information requirements. Many competitive intelligence units have failed because of their almost single-minded focus on gathering more and more of the data and information they believed managers should have or 'would be interested in'. An intelligence function that is not user-driven will fail. It will fail its immediate customers, the men and women charged with charting the course of the firm, and will therefore fail in its mission to inform strategic innovation and policy. Finally, it will not succeed in gaining company-wide support for the function and will therefore fail organizationally.

COLLECTION

Collection, or intelligence-gathering, is the second phase in the intelligence cycle. Collection requirements dictate how the intelligence unit will acquire the raw data and information that is needed. As part of its collection management responsibilities, the intelligence unit must determine when and from which sources it will obtain the information needed, who will be tasked with which specific collection responsibilities, and the most suitable format for delivery to analysts.

Analysts and collectors jointly set collection strategies as part of collection planning and operations. They must then 'implement that strategy by tasking personnel and resources to exploit selected sources, perform the collection, reformat the results if necessary to make them usable in the next stages, and forward the information to the intelligence production unit' (Krizan, 1999).

There are two especially important considerations when making the tough choices involved in developing collection priorities:

1. Alternative sources of information have proven to be inadequate. Intelligence should not concern itself with confirming or duplicating information already available from market research, the Internet or other sources readily accessible to, and usually already exploited by, managers.

2. The information required is unlikely to become available through means other than a systematic intelligence effort.

It is well known that government and the military have a much wider range of sources available to them than is typically the case in industry. These sources fall into five broad categories:

1. *Human-source intelligence (HUMINT)*. This generally refers to human sources outside the company, including competitor personnel, customers and suppliers as well as subject-matter experts, industry analysts, etc. Human sources are targeted for their knowledge and 'referral' to other sources

2. *Imagery intelligence (IMINT)*. This refers to both ground and overhead imagery, of which there are several categories. These include aerial photography, electro-optical imagery, imagery radar and infrared sensors. In the military, IMINT is the only discipline that allows commanders to 'see the battlefield' in real time as operations progress.

3. *Measurement and signature intelligence (MASINT)*. This refers to technically derived intelligence data other than IMINT or signals intelligence. It is commonly regarded in the US intelligence community as technically derived intelligence (excluding traditional imagery and signals intelligence) which, when collected, processed and analysed, results in intelligence that detects, tracks, identifies or describes the signatures (distinctive characteristics) of fixed or dynamic target sources (e.g. electromagnetic energy, sound, chemical and material residues).

4. *Open-source information*. This includes information available in the public domain. This can be anything from a newspaper article or web page to non-proprietary company documents. For the most part it comprises that

which companies themselves are prepared to release, as well as assessments of public domain information from industry observers. Open-source information provides the necessary starting point for any intelligence investigation and will usually point to a wide array of potential human sources, but in and of itself does not constitute intelligence.

5. *Signals intelligence (SIGINT)*. Information derived from intercepted communications, radar and telemetry. SIGINT can be regarded a 'bridge' between imagery's ability to observe activity and HUMINT's ability to gauge intentions. SIGINT, in short, provides a hedge against strategic deception and is useful in support of other collection assets.

The practice of competitive intelligence is limited mainly to open-source and HUMINT, although a company's counterintelligence and security staff should be especially concerned with the threats posed by SIGINT in terms of economic and industrial espionage. Our focus here, however, is on open-source and HUMINT collection disciplines.

Many competitive intelligence units continue to devote (waste?) a disproportionate amount of their efforts and resources in gathering overwhelming mountains of 'open'- rather than human-source information. This seldom results in anything meaningful in terms of unique intelligence product. Open-source information, in other words, will seldom reveal much about competitor or other key player commitment, thinking and intentions.

The Internet is a powerful enabling technology, but from an intelligence perspective it has far more in common with Pandora's box than it does with the perpetually elusive pot of intelligence gold. Open-source information represents the level playing field – it offers no inherent competitive advantage, hence the reason executives instinctively rely on their personal ('old boy'?) networks of friends and contacts at investment banks, strategy consulting firms and elsewhere for 'real' intelligence – not, unfortunately, on company internal sources usually perceived as less credible. In fact, an obsession with gathering public domain and 'private source' information poses something of a real threat to the underlying purpose of intelligence – as one former British intelligence officer observes: 'Not everything can be seen from satellites' (Herman, 1996).

So what does this mean for company intelligence programmes? Quite simply, an intelligence product that does not include a significant human-source intelligence (HUMINT) component is unlikely to provide managers with the knowledge-based competitive advantage they need and expect.

If a company's intelligence function is to be effective – if it is to succeed in its objective to generate a unique stream of products designed to provide executives with the estimates they need in order to plan for the future – competitive intelligence units must orient (or re-orient) the main thrust of collection efforts toward HUMINT. Although raw HUMINT represents essentially 'soft', often biased, information, and is 'vulnerable to errors and lies, to deception and self-deception' (Kovaks, 1997), it nevertheless offers a number of critically important advantages over open-source information. Human-source intelligence:

■ can provide 'decisive' confirmation or verification of intelligence obtained by other means;

■ goes beyond numbers and is largely qualitative;

■ provides prima facie evidence of rivals' motives, intentions, plans and deceptions;

■ reveals information hidden, or denied, from other forms of surveillance or monitoring.

But easier said than done. The collection of HUMINT requires that 'collectors' – the 'ground soldiers' of competitive intelligence and counterintelligence operations – possess finely honed competencies in elicitation and related 'social' skills. Elicitation, of course, is the art of obtaining information from human sources without disclosing the information objectives. Indeed, 'elicitation is perhaps the most valuable weapon in the intelligence collector's arsenal, and should rank highly in [company] intelligence training programmes' (Bernhardt, 1999). The art of elicitation (and counter-elicitation) can be taught, and must certainly be embedded as an essential part of any competitive intelligence training programme.

PROCESSING AND EXPLOITATION

Processing refers to the conversion of raw data to forms usable by intelligence analysts and others. Since intelligence deliverables are tailored to meet the specific needs of predetermined users, raw 'intelligence' derived from sources such as industry and market studies, news articles and rumours are usually unsuitable for decision-makers' consumption. Processing and exploitation involve activities such as the 'translation' or interpretation of press releases and technical reports, the drafting of commentary from 'interviews' – especially elicitation transcripts – and the collation of information. Collation will include

gathering, arranging, and annotating related information; drawing tentative conclusions about the relationship of 'facts' to each other and their significance; evaluating the accuracy and reliability of each item [of information]; grouping items into logical categories; critically examining the information source; and assessing the meaning and usefulness of the content for further analysis.

(Krizan, 1999)

Put differently, the processing of intelligence involves the following:

- *Testing for reliability of sources, in particular human sources.* For example: is a source new or well known to collectors? If well known, how reliable has he/she proven to be in the past? What access does the source have to the information? How far is he/she removed from the raw data?

- *Assigning confidence levels to the information.* That is, how much confidence do analysts attach to the information concerned? Does it make sense? Does it correspond with other 'knowns'?

- *Resolution of inconsistencies.* Information gathered as part of an intelligence collection exercise seldom falls neatly into place to create the perfect picture. Data or 'evidence' that does not quite fit the apparent pattern needs to be revisited and revalidated. Not infrequently the 'truth' is represented by the anomalies rather than the norm.

ANALYSIS AND PRODUCTION

Analysis is sometimes regarded as the 'black box' of intelligence activity. It is, in fact, the key driver of intelligence collection operations, and involves 'the process of evaluating and transforming raw data into descriptions, explanations, and conclusions for intelligence consumers' (Berkowitz and Goodman, 1989). The aim of competitive analysis is 'to help analysts, strategists, managers, and decision makers to make sense of the environment and of their organisations' evolving and dynamic position within it' (Fleisher and Bensoussan, 2002).

Long experience suggests that intelligence analysis serves its users best when the focus is on one or more of the following values:

- opportunities and threats, especially unexpected developments that may require management action or reaction;

- motives, plans, intentions, strengths and vulnerabilities of rivals and other key players;

- tactical alternatives, or options available, for advancing the organization's goals.

Figure 5.2 illustrates where 'value-added analysis' fits in the intelligence process. It is the last step before generating intelligence 'products' or reports.

There are very special challenges associated with intelligence analysis. The guidelines proposed by the CIA's Directorate of Intelligence are as valid in the business domain as they are in the national security context, and may be summarized as follows (CIA, 2002a):

■ 'Support the policymaking process without engaging in policymaking per se. The "if, then" approach can facilitate close policy support without crossing the line to policy prescription.'

■ 'Long-shot threats and opportunities.' Decision-makers 'often have a strong interest in low-probability, high-impact dangers and objectives ... [Intelligence] analysis in support of policymaking in these circumstances should provide expert, tough-minded assessments that concentrate, not on *whether* an event is likely, but *how* and *why* it might come about ...'

■ 'Pointing is not choosing.' That is to say, at times intelligence analysts must 'identify and clarify the vulnerabilities of adversaries and the sources of [the company's] leverage' over partners and third parties as well as competitors.

■ 'The timeliness challenge.' When executives 'are engaged in managing day-to-day crises, they will use whatever information is available to them when a decision point comes.' Put another way, delivering 'the best we've got' on time is better than disseminating a 'perfect' product too late.

Fig. 5.2 **Another view of the all-source intelligence process**

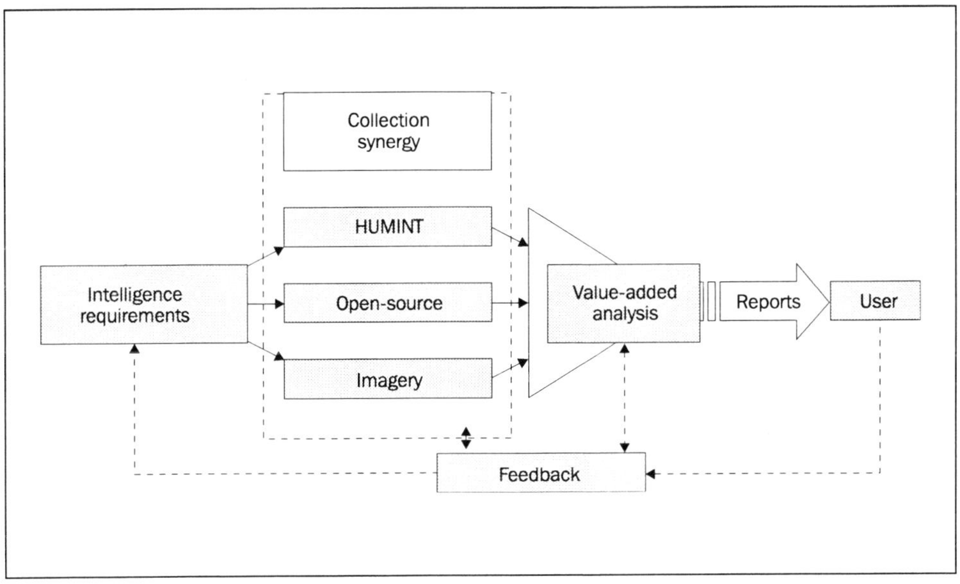

Adapted from a framework originally developed by SRA International Inc., Fairfax, Virginia

A high-level perspective on the roles and responsibilities of security intelligence and information analysis is illustrated in a model (*see* Figure 5.3) that we have adapted from one suggested by the US Office of Homeland Security.

This model reflects and reinforces 'the concept that intelligence and information analysis is not a separate, stand-alone activity but rather an integral component of [an organization's] overall effort to protect against and reduce [its] vulnerability' to competitive threats (Office of Homeland Security, 2002). It is not a 'black box' of shadowy tricks to be used when more conventional efforts to close critical information gaps have failed to produce results. A review of the key elements of the model is instructive when considering not only what intelligence involves, but how it relates to subsequent decisions and actions.

Fig. 5.3 Roles and responsibilities of security intelligence and information

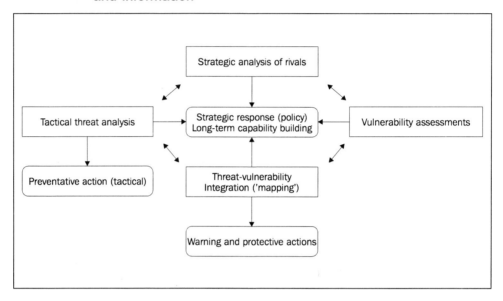

Strategic analysis of rivals

Knowledge of the current and future capabilities, ambitions and vulnerabilities of competitors supports longer-term strategies for defeating or gaining competitive advantage over rivals

Vulnerability assessments

Vulnerability assessments allow companies to better assess the consequences of possible competitor initiatives, and thereby strengthen defences against such threats

Tactical threat analysis

This is particularly important in helping to disrupt, sometimes prevent or minimize the impact of near-term competitor actions that may jeopardize company operations.

What, for example, is the likely impact of a rival's new sales campaign on our own sales performance and what are our response options?

Because intelligence analysis deals mainly with the future – about which there can be no data – it is sometimes wrong. What is important is that it is credible. Intelligence analysis must therefore demonstrate sound and logical reasoning, must articulate key assumptions, should, within the limits of security considerations, provide the sources of the 'facts' and, finally, offer conclusions upon which decisions and action can be taken.

DISSEMINATION

Dissemination involves the distribution of finished intelligence to users, the very same decision-makers whose needs drive the intelligence requirements from the beginning. Dissemination is also the weakest link in the intelligence cycle.

Finished intelligence should at all times be delivered in the format preferred by the recipient, tailored to conform to his or her preferences. Some managers digest information best in bullet-point presentations; others prefer comprehensive, detailed reports with all supporting evidence. It is up to intelligence staff to know their customers and their individual decision-making styles. For example, are their respective styles decisive? flexible? hierarchic? integrative?

Ideally intelligence should be classified in terms of the extent of damage the firm is likely to suffer if the information were to become public or end up in the hands of rivals. This means, too, only personnel cleared for a particular level of classification should be permitted access to intelligence product.

We advise company intelligence teams that effective intelligence dissemination involves four key factors:

1. *Oral delivery.* This is how intelligence analysts can be most certain of bringing to light what the user really needs to know. The results from the dialogue and feedback that takes place between intelligence staff and their customers when meeting face to face

2. *Inclusion of intelligence reports from the field.* Local assessments of intelligence issues or problems add considerable credibility to analysis completed by a central intelligence department. It helps answer the question: 'How do you know?'

3. *Laying out the evidence.* Decision-makers value seeing evidence that supports analysis and conclusions. The intelligence consumer is, in practice, the ultimate analyst, and in most cases will anyway exercise that privilege.

4. *Inclusion of optional actions and implications.* What actions might decision-makers wish to consider taking? What are the implications? And so on.

Unfortunately the smooth functioning of the intelligence process, from identifying intelligence needs through to dissemination, is rarely a straightforward matter. Historically, most so-called 'intelligence failures' can be attributed to a failure in dissemination. There are four main reasons for this:

- *A natural 'disconnect' between intelligence users* (typically seasoned 40–55-year-old 'experts' on everything regarding their company, their industry, their functional specialization and usually the world at large) *and the intelligence producer* (typically bright, analytically oriented subject experts or MBA-types not yet seasoned enough to 'know everything' about their company, their industry, or indeed the world at large).

- *Bureaucracy and culture* – or 'shooting ourselves in the foot'. Although the intelligence, per se, exists, internal organizational barriers (departmental silos, reporting lines, politics, etc.) impede the intelligence from reaching the right users on time. In many corporations disparities in rank, viewpoints and personality seem to matter more than making money.

- *Politicization*. The intelligence analysis is biased, or manipulated in some way to serve a 'personal' or departmental agenda. As Robert Gates, former US Director of Central Intelligence, once put it: 'The usual response of a policymaker to intelligence with which he disagrees or which he finds unpalatable is to ignore it.'

- *Security*. The user is not 'cleared' or is not offered access to the information. Quite simply, he or she is not 'in the loop'.

- *Technical*. A technical hitch in the system prevents the user from access to the intelligence. The intelligence is 'stuck in the system'.

Intelligence that fails to reach its intended user in a timely manner is of no value, regardless of how thorough the research or elegant to rigorous the analysis. The production of intelligence does not end with its collection and analysis – Pearl Harbour and 'September 11th' should have taught us that – it must be delivered to decision-makers as part of well coordinated dissemination procedures.

Intelligence products:
the 'deliverables'

INTRODUCTION

Ultimately it is the finished intelligence 'product' which serves as the actionable instrument for management decision-making. But just what is an intelligence 'product'? What are its attributes? What distinguishes it from the more conventional forms of management information? What are the different types?

The intelligence product, not unlike a product of any description, must match the needs and preferences of its customer as closely as possible. It must, in other words, highlight the internal customer's 'bottom-line' interests and requirements. Thus the quality of an intelligence product is measured in terms of its accuracy (which can only be fully assessed 'after the event'), its relevance to the original requirement and its timeliness. Executives are largely unconcerned with the 'magic' or processes that underpin it.

The key features of intelligence which is both useful and usable are the following:

- The intelligence user is involved from the beginning. His or her needs and expectations are clearly understood at the outset of the 'cycle'. In practice, this essentially becomes a function of the 'producer'–'consumer' dialogue or relationship that exists between intelligence and management.

- Intelligence findings are explicitly linked to the consumer's responsibilities. It makes no sense to prepare an intelligence report for, say, the marketing director when only the general manager of a specific business unit can act on it.

- It is predictive rather than passive. The future and likely developments are included.

- Implications for the company are fully discussed and assessed.

- Recommendations are made regarding the ongoing monitoring of key findings.

- The scope of the product – that is, 'both the amount of material it contains and the depth of coverage it provides on the topic' (Krizan, 1999) – is appropriate for the circumstances and corresponds to the user's requirements

Intelligence products must meet various tests of usability. These can be thought of in terms of the metrics shown in Table 6.1.

Table 6.1 Intelligence metrics

Real time – is the intelligence	Post facto – was the intelligence
Coherent?	Accurate?
Relevant?	Comprehensive?
Timely?	Predictive?
Unambiguous?	

Although a company's competitive intelligence department will, over time, develop its own formats corresponding to 'what works' for its internal customers, it is instructive to think in terms of the following five generic categories of finished intelligence – the same categories used by the US intelligence community:

1. current intelligence;
2. estimative intelligence;
3. research intelligence;
4. scientific and technical intelligence;
5. warning intelligence.

The sections which follow examine these categories in further detail.

CURRENT INTELLIGENCE

Current intelligence is usually prepared against a manager's, or management team's, explicit requirements and has a clearly defined end-date. Its main purpose is to provide managers with substantive, timely indications of new developments likely to have an impact on company strategy or operations. It addresses day-to-day events, and seeks to inform managers 'of new developments and related background, to assess their significance, to warn of their near-term consequences, and to signal potentially dangerous situations in the near future' (Office of Public Affairs, 1999).

Consider an instance in the pharmaceutical industry: knowledge of an unusually high incidence of serious side effects being experienced with a competitor's compound in clinical trials may well have an impact on a company's own drug development plans. The intelligence task is to determine the extent of the problem, with supporting detail and analysis of the implications for the competitor's development programme. The responsibility of managers is to consider how, if at all, the firm's drug development or marketing strategy for their own compound might be recalibrated.

Current intelligence is disseminated in a variety of formats, but will typically include the following headings:

-   Key judgments
-   Scope
-   Introduction
-   Evidence/findings
-   Implications.

Examples of current intelligence products are as follows:

- *CEO's daily brief (CDB)*. The CDB addresses intelligence issues of the highest significance necessary for the chief executive officer to perform his or her duties to advance the strategic goals and objectives of the organization as well as safeguard its security. It is an 'eyes only' product distributed to the CEO and sometimes other pre-selected members of the executive management team.

- *Senior executive intelligence briefing (SEIB)*. The SEIB is a compilation of current KITs. It is tailored to the needs those of executive and senior vice president rank, and is distributed several times a week.

- *Competitive intelligence assessment*. This is an in-depth analysis of a strategically relevant development, event, issue or situation in, say, 5 to 25 pages. It provides the decision-maker with evaluation and judgments. It is produced mainly for managers responsible for planning and policy, and is demand driven. It is the deliverable usually associated with an 'intelligence project' assigned to the CI unit.

ESTIMATIVE INTELLIGENCE

An intelligence estimate is the most authoritative analytic product prepared by a company's intelligence unit. It is a comprehensive analysis which includes long-range forecasts of key trends and their future implications for the organization. It is usually compiled at the direction of senior management for the purpose of helping executives envision the future – in particular the threats and opportunities – the company is likely to face. Its purpose is to minimize the risk of major policy failure by reducing decision-makers' uncertainties about the external environment, in effect helping decision-makers 'better appreciate the true state of the world and the hazards and opportunities' confronting the organization (Ford, 1993). It deals, in short, with the big, strategic questions, and spans departmental, functional and geographic boundaries. Intelligence estimates provide senior executives with the headlamps they need to seek through the fog and darkness that otherwise conceal 'the road ahead'.

Typically, the 'outlook' section of an intelligence estimate will assess the likely course and impact of important industry, market, scientific and technological developments, and 'identify the dynamics that will have the greatest impact on subsequent developments' (CIA, 2002b). What, for example, 'are the drivers that will determine the outcome, or what drivers would have to change to alter the outcome?' (CIA, 2002b).

The topic of an intelligence estimate will deal with problems and questions of concern to the corporation's most senior executives. Thus it will represent:

- the compilation of all relevant data and information – from human, open and other sources – that the CI unit possesses on the question;

- the examination of the data and information by an intelligence team, who then make corresponding estimative judgments;

- a description 'of the principal forces at work in the given question under examination' (CIA, 2002b).

Intelligence estimates, therefore, offer forecasts or predictions about the future, often years ahead, and as such tend to reflect the best judgments of the company's intelligence analysts. Unfortunately, in a business environment driven by the short-term pressures of satisfying today's investment community wolf packs of analysts, integrating estimative intelligence into a firm's strategic thinking requires a far more disciplined approach than most companies can honestly claim to possess.

RESEARCH INTELLIGENCE

Research intelligence involves in-depth studies generally presented in the form of confidential, highly-focused monographs or memorandums. It underpins current and estimative intelligence and is of two types.

Basic research intelligence

This is research and analysis on key regional, market, competitor and political events or topics. Basic research intelligence is sometimes used by decision-makers to support new initiatives or is sometimes stored in anticipation of future 'crises'. Consider, for example, a case where a European manufacturer of heavy-duty gas turbines believes that an American competitor is 'unfairly' benefiting from indirect US government subsidies for technology development. Management might task its intelligence team to investigate the matter and report by way of a detailed, analytical monograph.

Research intelligence also involves the preparation of what are commonly referred to as 'competitor profiles'. The idea, of course, is not to recast that which is readily available from open sources – such as Hoover's Online for instance – but rather to validate key data and assumptions held about a competitor, combined with a 'so what' analysis of what the information means.

Operational support intelligence

This is tailored, focused and rapidly produced intelligence to satisfy the needs of managers with operational responsibilities. Country, sales force and channel marketing managers would be typical users. Here intelligence may be asked to investigate topics such as: 'What changes in the competitor's sales force composition or size are being planned?' 'What does the competitor's new training programme for its distributors involve?'

SCIENTIFIC AND TECHNICAL INTELLIGENCE

Scientific and technical (S&T) intelligence is critically important for firms in science- or technology-based industries. Even in more traditional industries it is necessary to have an understanding of rivals' process technologies, especially where improvements in a competitor's efficiency could substantially improve their cost advantages.

Two industries where some of the biggest investments in intelligence capabilities are made are pharmaceuticals and telecommunications. Here the job of intelligence often centres as much around the 'whys' as the 'whats' and 'hows'. Learning from conventional sources that a firm is taking a particular technology direction is seldom difficult. The big question often is 'why are they doing that?' 'What do they know, or what assumptions do they hold that we do not, and what are the implications'?

Two American experts in technology intelligence suggest five 'reasons why technology is a natural focus of intelligence activities in business' (Ashton and Klavans, 1997):

1. Technology is a basic determinant of a company's competitive position.
2. New technology can be acquired from many global sources.
3. It can be a direct source of business revenue.
4. Technology eventually becomes obsolete, sometimes quite rapidly, and emerging technology from external sources in not always 'visible' to outsiders.
5. Technology information can have a substantial intelligence value in assessing a competitor's future business position because it is one of the earliest opportunities to gain insight into next-generation products and processes.

WARNING INTELLIGENCE

The subject of warning intelligence is discussed in Chapter 4. Warning products do, however, take several forms, two of which are described below.

Warning watchlist

This takes the form of a regular report that tracks and assigns probabilities to potential threats to the company's strategic interests or security that may develop within a fixed time frame, e.g. three to six months.

Warning alert

This communicates warning intelligence that warrants immediate attention on the part of company decision-makers. The warning may concern issues of corporate, business unit or regional concern and would be disseminated to the appropriate executives. A 'warning alert' should include:

- statement of facts;
- analysis and outlook;
- implications for the firm;
- intelligence gaps;
- possible actions.

SO WHAT SHOULD EXECUTIVES BE ASKING FOR?

Several years ago Kevin Sharer, chairman and CEO of Amgen, the world's largest biotechnology company, addressed this issue at a Chicago conference of the Society of Competitive Intelligence Professionals. At the time of the presentation he was executive vice president and president of the Business Markets Division of MCI Communications. Sharer also served as a US Naval officer on two nuclear fast-attack submarines during the Cold War. He put it this way:

> *So, how do I like to get intelligence? I like to get it fast and I like to understand the facts. Facts can be a lot of things. They can be analytic evaluation of cost structure, market research, or what the salesperson tells you. Every time I am listening to someone, I have one question going through my mind – so what? When you call on me, within one minute I'm starting to form conclusions about whether I want to keep talking to you or not.*
>
> *So, I want it fast, I want it factual, I want it integrated. Please don't come out of a wheelbarrow and say, 'Hey, look what I got! I got all these jigsaw puzzle parts,' and dump them down on my carpet and sit there and try to guess with me what sort of picture it makes. Please, put the puzzle together before you see me.*
>
> *I want it actionable, too. That's interesting, so what? You don't need to make cosmic predictions. You've gone out, you've collected information, you've reflected, and your view is that we are 95% right in what we are doing. But here's a little course correction we could make.*
>
> *… Come at me in a way that's different. Come in and say, 'Hello, this is a presentation of how it must today look to your counterpart at your leading competitor. Here's how the world must look to that person. Here's what*

actions I would be willing to bet they will take in the next three months and why. Here's what we should do about them.' That's a creative approach.

Try to think two steps ahead. Something in the world is happening now. We're going to take action. What action is the other guy going to take? That's as far ahead as anybody can think competitively. We need to understand their history to be able to predict their actions.'

(Sharer, 1990)

Executives need to consider four things when requesting specific items of intelligence or tasking the intelligence staff with the monitoring of a warning topic:

1. What is it that I need to know?
2. How will I use it? What decision will it support?
3. How do I like it presented? What format works for me?
4. When do I need it by?

Our aim here, quite simply, has been to demonstrate that there is no one form of intelligence deliverable. Intelligence products are as varied as are the issues they address and the 'consumers' they are designed to serve. The challenge, as always, is to package and deliver 'product' that makes a profound difference to the customer and the effectiveness with which he or she meets the challenges of management decision-making.

Intelligence organization

INTRODUCTION

In our consulting practice we are often compelled to remind managers that it was more than 20 years ago that Michael Porter, Professor of Business Administration at Harvard Business School, encouraged companies to address the need for 'an organised mechanism – some sort of competitor intelligence *system*' (Porter, 1980). For many firms, this has meant little more than appointing a 'token' manager of competitive intelligence, with the minimum of resources available to him or her, to run a function that in government, as well as in a relatively small – albeit growing – handful of firms, serves – or should serve! – as a 'first line of defence' against security threats. This begets the question: why? Why have companies been so reluctant to implant and nourish a competitive intelligence system in their firms? The obvious answer, the answer that repeatedly surfaces as a core problem of intelligence, is one that should be giving shareholders and employees alike more than a few sleepless nights: decision-makers are reluctant, and will often refuse, to consider information that does not conform to their view of the world or match their individual agendas. Put another way, they do not want to hear what they don't want to hear.

A competitive intelligence system does not comprise one or two bright-eyed, freshly minted MBAs – with annual resources amounting to a mere several hundred thousand euros – beavering away at corporate headquarters trying to decipher the 'meaning of life' (largely from what they download from the Internet). As US lawmakers concluded following a review of the counterterrorism capabilities and performance of the Intelligence Community before 11 September 2001, 'The terrorist attacks [in New York City and Washington, DC] constituted a significant strategic surprise for the United States. The failure of the Intelligence Community to provide adequate forewarning was affected by resource constraints and a series of questionable management decisions related to funding priorities' (US Subcommitte on Terrorism, 2002). Sound familiar? Ask yourself: just how much is our company willing to invest every year to reduce the risk of strategic surprise? As much as we spend on advertising? On paper clips?

A competitive intelligence system, as described by Jan Herring, is 'the organizational means by which information is systematically collected, analysed, and disseminated as intelligence to users (that is, the appropriate corporate management and staffs) who can act on it' (Herring, 1996). It is the only function in a firm – unlike technology development, operations, marketing and sales, and others – which has no stake in the outcome of a decision. The purpose of a CI department or unit is to manage the intelligence cycle or process and all its aspects as routinely as a company manages its accounting, logistics and other systems. More bluntly: it exists to ensure that intelligence helps save managers (and their organization) from themselves.

There is no one standardized competitive intelligence system. As with any system, CI must be in alignment with the architecture of the organization of which it is a part, and at all levels. It is a mechanism which exists to:

- develop and maintain current profiles – including personality profiles – of key industry players, and anticipate their likely behaviour;
- keep managers and other internal customers informed about developments and realities in the external business environment necessary for more intelligent decision-making;
- provide decision-makers with analytically derived assessments and estimates about future developments and explanations about their implications for strategy, operations and plans;
- equip executives with information and analysis not available through other channels.

BENEFITS OF A COMPETITIVE INTELLIGENCE SYSTEM

Intelligence, not unlike any other organizational activity, must deliver benefits. A competitive intelligence system exists to support future-oriented decision-making and actions for all primary and support elements of the firm's value chain – the collection of discrete activities in which competitive advantage resides at all organizational levels (corporate, divisional, regional, business unit, etc.). Competitive intelligence can well make the defining difference in the outcome of acquisitions, product and technology development, and marketing strategies and more.

Specific benefits include:

- improved productivity, or leveraging, of the firm's knowledge assets (thereby serving as a driver of increased shareholder value);
- early warning of competitive threats;
- a unique source of unbiased news, truth and analysis relevant to strategic and operational decision-making;
- improved cross-functional relationships throughout the organization;
- provision of ongoing linkages with security (and ideally counterintelligence);
- reinforcement of a 'culture' of competitiveness in the firm by focusing on external threats and influences.

What are the characteristics of a 'world-class' CI system? It is, above all, demand driven. The intelligence process, and its output, are driven in response to user requirements, whether explicitly articulated by users or anticipated by the CI team as part of their responsibility to stay abreast of important strategic concerns and issues. In addition:

- Intelligence deliverables are high value-added products. They provide 'analysis that helps [managers] to develop a sound picture of the world, to list the possible ways to achieve their action goals, and to influence others to accept their visions' (Gardiner, 1989).

- The company's intelligence heads have ready, informal access to the CEO, and enjoy his or her full confidence as well as the confidence of other senior leaders in the organization.

- An effective human-source intelligence (HUMINT) capability exists – and represents an integral part of collection activities.

- An efficient 'strategic early warning system' is in place, which concentrates on the earliest possible identification of changes in the external environment that may adversely affect company interests.

- Senior managers 'proactively' task their intelligence unit with intelligence requirements, and integrate intelligence input into their decision-making processes.

- Intelligence evolves into a core competence of the firm.

Few companies today can claim they meet all the above criteria. Most firms, it appears, demonstrate a propensity to 'manage risk' rather than initiate the gathering and analysis of evidence that helps anticipate it.

MISSION OF AN INTELLIGENCE DEPARTMENT

Companies everywhere create mission statements in order to make the organizational purpose explicit, and hopefully mobilize the thinking, spirits and actions of employees around that mission. For example, when Amazon.com started its operations in July 1995 it declared its mission would be 'to use the Internet to transform book buying into the fastest, easiest, and most enjoyable shopping experience possible.' Amazon.com was evidently serious about its purpose: the company's total sales – books, music, DVDs and more – are now around $4 billion and growing. As a further example, the mission of Nokia Corporation's Nokia Ventures Organization (NVO) – a separate division – is 'to push the limits of Nokia's growth beyond the scope of current businesses by introducing and developing new business ideas'. By early 2002 NVO's $650 million venture partners fund had already funded more than 30 early-stage mobile technology companies.

Similarly, it is essential that there exists a clear articulation of the mission of a firm's competitive intelligence organization. The 'mission statement' below was developed not as an attempt to create the definitive expression of the mission of intelligence, but rather as a guideline – in part based on the US national security model – that may help companies frame their own specific CI mission statements:

We support the chief executive officer, the senior management team, and others responsible for making and executing organizational strategy, policy and plans by:

- providing accurate, evidence-based, relevant and timely intelligence related to company goals and objectives; and

- conducting counterintelligence activities and other functions related to intelligence and corporate security, as directed by management.

OPERATIONS AND PLANS

The basic operational and functional activities and responsibilities of a competitive intelligence organization are depicted in Figure 7.1.

Fig. 7.1 Basic operational and functional activities and responsibilities of a competitive intelligence organization

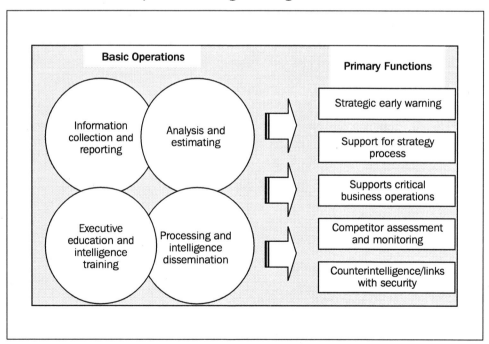

WHERE TO BEGIN

When a company decides to introduce or upgrade a CI system, it must first start with an intelligence audit. The audit process, which is often facilitated by a specialized consulting firm, is illustrated in Figure 7.2.

Fig. 7.2 Intelligence audit process

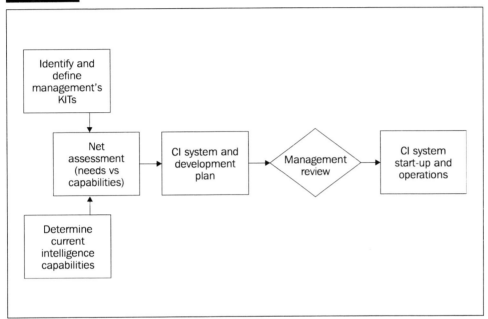

The intelligence audit involves:

■ the identification of current and future intelligence requirements – KITs – of the company's executive management team and key functional and operations managers;

■ an assessment of the company's existing intelligence collection and analysis capabilities (competencies, practices, resources, IT systems);

■ the design of a system corresponding to the company's specific business model and organizational architecture, and its future intelligence needs.

The results of the audit lead not only the preparation of a CI system design but also to an implementation plan. The plan – which should specify necessary processes, structure, personnel training needs and the like – is then reviewed by management for approval and start-up.

STRUCTURE

Figure 7.3 provides a simplified, generic example of how a CI department might be organized at a divisional or business unit level depending upon the specific organizational culture and set-up of the company.

Fig. 7.3 Example of a CI department organization

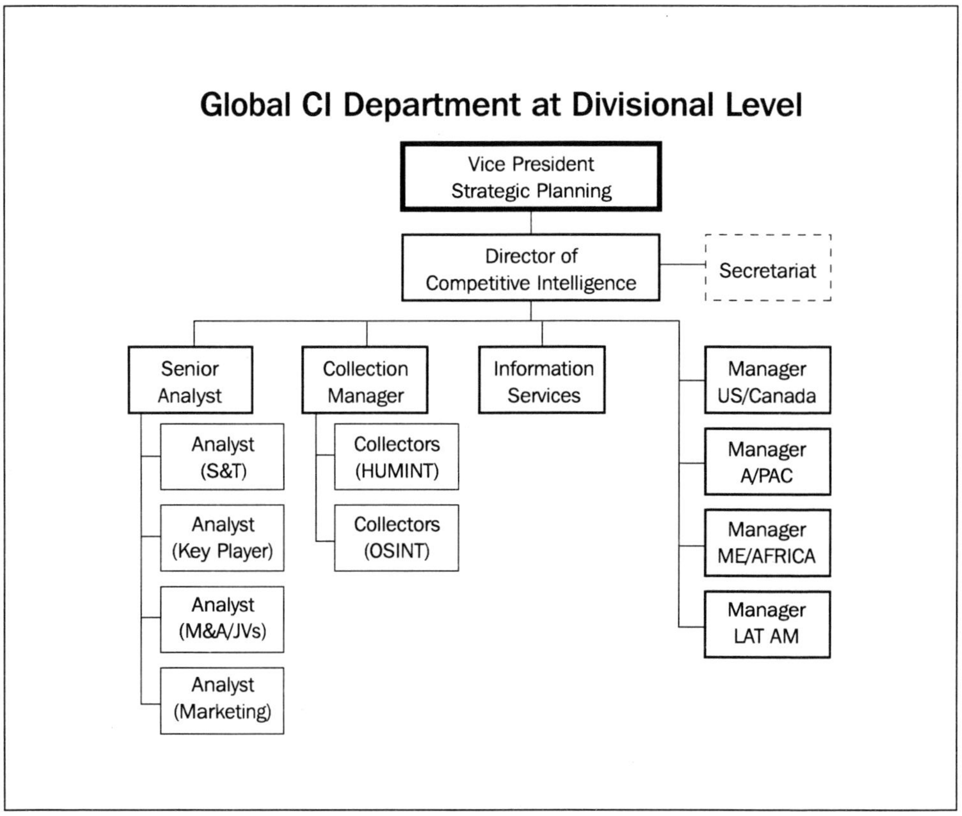

Global CI Department at Divisional Level

In this model the regional CI heads are shown reporting directly to the Director of Competitive Intelligence (DCI) rather than local general managers. In practice this is seldom the case; the regional CI managers' links with the divisional director is usually 'dotted line'. Unfortunately, in such instances, bureaucratic impediments are likely to reduce efficiencies in speed, effectiveness and, most importantly, objectivity of analysis and reporting.

The responsibilities of the CI department are most easily understood in terms of the intelligence cycle, and thus involve:

- defining and interpreting KITs for collection planning;
- collection management and all-source collection activities;
- analysis and preparation of intelligence products;
- dissemination to internal users.

Various ancillary responsibilities involve training and education, process development and coordination, and counterintelligence.

One of the earlier studies of CI systems was carried out by Ben Gilad (1991), at the time an Associate Professor of Management at Rutgers University, in Newark, New Jersey. Gilad drew parallels between intelligence as applied in the national security environment and in the corporate arena. Table 7.1 is adapted from his description.

Table 7.1 Gilad's national security intelligence model

	Non-business environment	Corporate environment
Objective	Support head of state and cabinet members	Support CEO and top management team
Justification	Free political decision-makers to form and execute foreign policy	Free executives to form and executive competitive strategy
Organization	Independent, professional function; director reporting to president/prime minister	Corporate-level function or SBU-level position of equal rank with finance, HR, marketing, etc.; director reporting to CEO or SBU head
Internal Division	Collection and research separated	Depending on resources, analysts may combine roles
Sources	Agents/officers in the field; open sources; signals, photo, imagery and other electronic intelligence	Internal experts; consultants; published sources; Internet
Interface with Decision-makers	Director sits in on cabinet/'security council' meetings, advisory committees; experts participate in briefings and hearings	CEO and top management set direction and priorities; intelligence function provides decision intelligence, issue intelligence
Scope	Military, political, economic, science and technology	Competitors, customers, suppliers, regulatory agencies and other key players; acquisitions, technology, socio-economic
Contribution to Leader	Facts, estimates, understanding, questions, sensitization	Same

Adapted from Gilad (1991).

No manager or company would question the necessity for functions such as accounting or marketing. Yet the notion of an intelligence function still remains a 'hard sell' in many firms, forced to compete for a few financial crumbs of budget while competitors outside manoeuvre like vultures to take advantage of any misstep or vulnerability. Unless and until companies take steps to embed a well funded, professionally managed CI function throughout their organization they will remain at a competitive disadvantage.

Ethics

The importance of the ethical considerations that attach to the practice of competitive intelligence is not to be underestimated. Often it is the question of ethics that presents managers and intelligence staff with their greatest personal as well as organizational dilemmas. While the objective of intelligence is to continuously seek information advantage for the firm, all organizations and individuals function within the context of ethical standards, however much such standards may vary from culture to culture, company to company and person to person.

Concern over ethical standards, as distinct from the matter of law (which concerns itself mainly with industrial espionage), is never far from the discussion agendas and debates of the directors and members of the Society of Competitive Intelligence Professionals (SCIP). Indeed, SCIP promotes a 'Code of Ethics' which endeavours to articulate the minimum set of ethical standards to which it expects CI practitioners to adhere. In addition, together with the Conference Board's Council on Competitive Analysis, SCIP has published a collection of corporate codes of conduct that are designed to serve as models for companies who wish to create, modify or revise their own ethical guidelines (SCIP, 1997).

BETTER SAFE THAN SORRY

Ethics has been defined as a subset of values concerned with the ends or principles of conduct. At SCIP's 1995 Annual Conference, Thomas Donaldson, Professor of Business Ethics at Georgetown University, Washington, DC, offered the following 'global guideposts' regarding ethics:

- Before judging, try to understand.
- When you hit a wall, seek a creative solution.
- Consider adopting an international 'issue management' process that identifies and resolves conflicts of culture and ethics.
- Remember that sometimes there is no compromise.
- Tailor ethics and values education to respect local differences.
- Let business units overseas contribute to the interpretation of ethical issues.
- In host countries support efforts to decrease institutional corruption.

In our work with companies worldwide, we have discovered that on many issues there is a wide disparity between individual managers and their firms about what is considered ethical and what is not. For example, there is no universal consensus on the ethics of eavesdropping (non-electronic) in public settings, the debriefing of former employees of competitors for non-proprietary information, reverse engineering or sifting through competitors' rubbish bins (so-called 'dumpster diving') when trespass is not involved. On the other hand it is generally accepted within the

European and North American business environments that the following practices are not ethical, whatever the legal position:

- bribing competitors, customers or suppliers for information;
- conducting illegitimate 'job interviews';
- eavesdropping or electronic surveillance ('bugging');
- hiring an employee away to get proprietary knowledge;
- interception of communications (data, fax, telephone, etc.);
- planting an agent on a competitor's payroll;
- posing as a customer, student, journalist or headhunter;
- trespassing on a competitor's property.

And, in any event, there seems to be general agreement that intelligence activities must remain firmly within the boundaries of the law. One problem, of course, is that what is perceived as ethical in one country or jurisdiction will be viewed quite differently in another. In some countries, for example, bribing one or more officials as part of the bidding or contract process is regarded as standard business practice and not illegal or unethical. This applies equally to information-gathering. Consider France. The French intelligence and security services have explicit responsibilities to protect and help advance the economic interests of France. Where the interests of a state-owned or other large French enterprise are concerned, in the eyes of the French – and the logic cannot, in fact, be faulted – it is perfectly natural that the intelligence services which are, after all, simply an arm of the state, lend support to those interests.

With ethics, as with philosophy, there is seldom, if ever, a 'right' answer. Nevertheless, the issue cannot be ignored. Especially today, when the spotlight on executive behaviour has never been brighter, companies must take steps to ensure that the practices of their intelligence units, as well as those of the consultants they engage, are carried out within acceptable boundaries of behaviour. The 'rules' associated with human-source intelligence collection in particular need to be clearly and explicitly defined.

All large firms have policies which specify what is acceptable (or expected) and what is not in terms of employee conduct. Intelligence staff and external consulting firms must be made aware of such policies, and must formally agree to be bound by them.

PRINCIPLES AND POLICY

John Prescott, Professor of Business Administration at the Joseph M. Katz Graduate School of Business, University of Pittsburgh, and a leading competitive intelligence academic, suggests certain 'basic principles for the development of a code of ethics that need to be institutionalized as part of your organization's culture'. These principles include the following:

- Deception such as posing as a journalist or business student should never be used.

- 'Undue influence' over employees, or prospective employees, who possess privileged competitor information must be avoided.

- Unsolicited proprietary information, such as a competitor's strategic or operating plans or confidential documents relating to processes or technologies, should be immediately turned over to your company lawyers.

We make three recommendations for action:

- The corporate legal department, in cooperation with the firm's head of competitive intelligence, should draft and disseminate a clear set of ethical guidelines. Anyone with an intelligence or counterintelligence responsibility – including consultants – should be made aware of, and required to abide by, and formally 'sign off' on, the guidelines.

- All intelligence and counterintelligence personnel should be encouraged to familiarize themselves with current legislation and any legal opinions, relevant to business intelligence processes and 'products'.

- Formal mechanisms must be put into place to regularly audit and evaluate organization-wide competitive intelligence operations.

All intelligence collection activities should be conducted with one overriding question in mind: 'Would we, and our customers, be happy to see what we've done reported on the front pages of the *Financial Times*?'

Counterintelligence: the other side of the coin

*The main body of this chapter has been written by **Steve Whitehead**, Managing Member of CBIA cc, South Africa's oldest competitive intelligence and counterintelligence consultancy. He is an executive member of the South African Association of Competitive Intelligence Professionals (SAACIP), South African Institute of Security (SAIS) and international associations such as Society of Competitive Intelligence Professionals (SCIP), American Society for Industrial Security (ASIS) and Business Espionage Controls & Countermeasures Association (BECCA). He speaks and writes regularly on the topic of the protection of business information.*

INTRODUCTION[1]

Consider for a moment a sports team – basketball, rugby or ice hockey, say – with a strategy for offence only and players trained exclusively in offensive tactics. Although the team's coach recognizes that in any game or match it is as important to prevent rivals from scoring as it is to score, he or she has not sought to develop the team's defensive capability. Of course this is a preposterous notion. Yet that is precisely the state of affairs at most companies today. While a corporate security department is as much a 'part of the furniture' as the accounting department at most medium-size and large-scale firms today, few if any companies possess a well-defined counterintelligence function. Although 'security' may represent a component of counterintelligence, the traditional responsibility of a company's security department for physical security has little to do with the risks associated with the loss – by theft or otherwise – of a firm's proprietary knowledge.

There is no one definition of counterintelligence. At a minimum, however, counterintelligence can be defined as the identification and neutralization of the threat posed by 'unfriendly' intelligence services, and the manipulation of those services for the manipulator's benefit. It is, in other words, that aspect of intelligence covering all activity which is devoted to eliminating or reducing the effectiveness of rivals' intelligence operations, and to the protection of proprietary information against economic and industrial espionage.

How ready is your company to protect its secrets and intellectual property? Indeed, how prepared are you to provide answers to the following three questions:

1. What are our competitors trying to discover about us, and why?

2. How are they trying to do it?

3. What countermeasures do we have in place to prevent it?

A number of things can happen to a company when proprietary information is 'leaked' or stolen. The greatest risk is that a company can go out of business if the basis for its competitive advantage is lost. When companies do not protect their critical information they will definitely lose market share, lose valuable know how and suffer damage to the name of their company and its brands, which in turn results in loss of confidence by investors, business associates and even their own managers and staff.

As this briefing has shown, many firms today go to great lengths to obtain information about their competitors. They can make use of legal/ethical, unethical and illegal information-gathering techniques or a combination to gather business secrets. Companies do not all abide by an ethics code and many misrepresent themselves or break laws to get information about their competitors.

Peter Hamilton, a highly regarded British security expert, has cautioned that: 'Industrial espionage poses a significant threat ... It will not be possible for any company or economy to survive the battle without good industrial intelligence. Organised industrial espionage would be a logical outcome of this need' (Hamilton, 1979).

The danger of industrial espionage is often underestimated as most of the time there are no overt signs or indications of the attack against a company, making it difficult to spot. In a 1999 article two British private investigators spoke about their tactics and methods to gather information: 'By day, dressed in business suits they posed as procurement agents' (*Fortune*, 6 September 1999).

Unsuspecting employees can cost companies millions. If any form of intelligence 'attack' – legal or illegal – is executed in a professional manner most companies are unlikely to notice. They usually only become aware of the problem when it is too late, e.g. a competitor unexpectedly launching products clearly based on one's own ideas or technologies.

Not many businesses are linking the collection of information or the attacks against confidential information with information protection or counterintelligence.

Corporate counterintelligence is necessary in an organized manner to protect a company's information and secrets. A counterintelligence capability and effective policies and procedure will add value and allow companies to compete with more confidence in the global marketplace.

Counterintelligence is an integral part of all the business activities in a company and the counterintelligence programmes must extend through all levels in the organization. In this regard the old saying 'prevention is better than cure' is specifically true.

HOW WIDESPREAD IS THE THREAT OF INFORMATION THEFT?

The selection of recent headlines and quotes given below indicate that information theft and industrial espionage could be a worldwide problem. It also seems that not much has changed regarding the second oldest profession, except the information requirements.

> *Tycoon faces charges of spying, fraud.*
> (*Kathimerini News*, Greece, 20 February 2002)

> *Corporate espionage is spreading rapidly in India, adversely affecting or threatening to affect businesses.*
> (*Indian Express*, 26 March 2001)

Indications are that economic espionage, including trade secret thefts and competitive business information/intelligence gathering, will intensify and be more aggressively pursued in the new millennium.

(Peter F. Kalitka, *Periscope*, March 2000)

China's spies target corporate America.

(*Fortune Magazine*, 30 March 1998)

Former CIA chief: business spy threat is real.

(CNN.com, 18 October 2000)

Experts say more companies are relying on professionals to scope out rivals.

(Estaban Parra, *News Journal*, 2 December 2001)

Snooping on the Reserve Bank.

(*Financial Mail*, South Africa, July 2001)

ESPIONAGE AND BUSINESS INTELLIGENCE

The US Attorney General's definition of economic espionage is 'the unlawful or clandestine targeting or acquisition of sensitive financial, trade, or economic policy information; proprietary economic information; or critical technologies' (NACIC Annual Report to USA Congress on Foreign Economic Collection and Industrial Espionage, 2000). The definition excludes the collection of open and legally available information.

The collection of information in an open and legal manner is referred to as competitive intelligence or business intelligence. Competitive intelligence is a coordinated effort in an organized manner to collect information about competitors, suppliers, customers and a specific industry to gain a competitive edge. The focus is, however, on the legal and ethical gathering of this information from secondary and primary sources.

WHAT DO COMPANIES NEED TO PROTECT?

The emphasis in trade has shifted to information and technology-based products. The trade in intellectual property is also becoming a greater component of world trade. Some describe it as the new global currency. Proprietary information is more and more recognized as a company's most valuable asset.

The information companies need to protect includes technological as well as financial and commercial information that gives them a competitive edge over their competitors.

One just has to look at the characteristics of information to understand why it is such a difficult thing to protect. Information can be something that is audible or visible (model, document, plan, etc.), or may be smelled, tasted and touched.

Intellectual property protects the innovation of a person's mind. At the end of the day this is where real power and real wealth lies. Intellectual property gives the owner an exclusive right, i.e. a competitive advantage.

Intellectual property has its own requirements for protection. It is necessary to scrutinize all the efforts of competitors, even their open-source collection efforts as this often leads to the discovery of other illegal activities against a company.

WHAT IS COUNTERINTELLIGENCE?

The most basic objective of counterintelligence is to protect information from those who are not authorized to receive it, to counter potential threats and to enhance security.

Counterintelligence should not only protect against aggressive and illegal information collection but also against open and legal collection efforts that can harm a company and affect its ability to compete in its market.

Counterintelligence programmes will spot the danger signals, foil industrial espionage, prevent illegal activities such as electronic eavesdropping, carefully control critical information that a company publishes about itself and protect those areas vulnerable to business intelligence and espionage efforts by making it difficult for competitors to collect information.

Counterintelligence is an important business task and has to be assigned to an individual(s) who understands intelligence principles, espionage and the stealthy attack methods employed by those who pry into corporate secrets.

Some definitions:

Counterintelligence is fundamentally directed at coping with or countering threat. This threat may be immediate, latent or potential.

(Arthur A. Zuehlke, Jr)

Counterintelligence must be seen in full perspective – as a vital element of a nation's security system, the essential underpinning not only of an effective foreign policy but for the protection of out free institutions as well.

(Newton S. Miler)

Counterintelligence's mission is to protect the entire entity – whether government or corporate – from outside or inside harm.

(Lawrence B. Sulc)

Counterintelligence has both passive and active components. Passive counterintelligence aims to counter what an adversary may do and comprises defensive and preventative countermeasures such as awareness briefings, technical surveillance countermeasures (TSCM) and penetration testing.

Active counterintelligence differs from passive counterintelligence. Once the threat or hostile entity has been detected and identified, active counterintelligence will investigate and conduct operations to eliminate any ongoing or threatening activity. When employed aggressively it is also a collection process. To be able to counter what an adversary may do counterintelligence needs reliable and good information about competitors' intentions, capabilities, budget and resources.

THE NEED FOR COUNTERINTELLIGENCE

In the contemporary world, business and commercial targets are becoming increasingly more important to foreign intelligence services than military or political targets.

Any company competing with foreign business in the international arena could be a target for corporate espionage. James Woolsey, while Director of Central Intelligence, reported that economics has become the hottest current topic in intelligence. Pierce Marcon, former head of the French Direction Générale de la Sécurité Extérieur (DGSE) said in an interview to an American television reporter, 'In economics we are competitors, not allies'. One of the tasks of the First Directorate of the Russian Foreign Intelligence Services (SVR) is international economics. The first chief of this directorate is an expert in international economic relations. The Japan External Trade Organization (JETRO), established in 1957 to promote trade under Japan's Ministry of International Trade and Industry (MITI), is considered by many western intelligence services as one of the world's best 'intelligence services'.

A company should know itself as well as its competitors. It should determine what information should be protected, its vulnerabilities and for how long the information or processes should be protected. A company that has strict standards of physical security can be devastated by a 'penetration agent', a staff member working for a competitor.

A company that does not practise information protection regarding its sensitive documents and records is vulnerable even if all of the staff are dedicated and loyal people. Excellent physical security and trustworthy personnel are not enough to protect a company from a dedicated intelligence or espionage effort against it.

The US Economic Espionage Act of 1996 led the way. The Act is an attempt by the US government to assist American businesses against industrial espionage from foreign intelligence services and information-gatherers. The Act also includes the term 'proprietary economic information' and links the economic well-being of American companies to national security. The Act empowers the FBI to assist American businesses.

The Act basically *prohibits* the taking, copying or receiving of trade secrets without authorization. It also prohibits anyone from doing so for the 'benefit' of any foreign government, foreign instrumentality or foreign agent.

The Act also requires that the owner of the information must have taken reasonable and active measures to *protect* the information from becoming known to unauthorized individuals. If owners fail to protect their information no one can be accused of misappropriation. The owner of the information would also not be able to claim relief under the Economic Espionage Act.

In many other countries the business sector does not enjoy the same protection and assistance from their respective governments that American businesses do and have to provide for their own protection against information theft and espionage.

ESPIONAGE METHODS AND MOTIVATIONAL FACTORS

Methods of espionage and motivational factors behind them include:

- trespassing;
- covert surveillance;
- electronic eavesdropping and bugging;
- trash collection (dumpster diving or trash analysis);
- burglaries;
- blackmail, bribery;
- stealing of documents;
- the threat from within which could be the recruitment of a staff member or the infiltration of an agent.

Probably the biggest threat is the 'penetration agent', a staff member working for a competitor. This allows the competitor access to records, files, documents, products, equipment, strategic plans, and customer and sales records to increase their competitive edge. The industrial spy will look for 'holes' to penetrate the business under attack. One such hole is of course the angry or dissatisfied employee.

But why do people spy and commit business espionage? The motives for spying or stealing of secrets are usually mixed and can be for material, emotional and/or ideological reasons. The motivation to spy could be caused by a deep dissatisfaction about status, insecurity, being a member of a minority group, being overly ambitious or fanatical or could also be caused by some obsession. Alcohol, drugs, gambling and sex are just a few of the vices that can easily turn into an obsession.

Money usually plays a big part in the corrupting of individuals but anger and revenge are motivational factors specifically where individuals have been passed over for promotion or felt that their contributions are not specifically recognized.

Financial problems, marital conflicts and excessive debts could all contribute to the motivation to spy for a competitor.

The industrial spy will usually conduct an operational 'analysis' of the company and staff targeted to find the best way and means to obtain the required information. The industrial spy may use a process called 'spotting' to locate, identify and collect information on the staff members who appear to be of potential value to his assignment. The spotting process will usually be carried out in such a manner that leaves the 'candidate' unaware of the spotting activity until the time that he or she is approached to spy against his or her own company. The threat of a penetration agent in one's own company can be greatly reduced by the implementation of counterintelligence measures that can deter or detect this kind of activity. Counterintelligence enables a company to identify the threats and the 'tradecraft' (collection methods) employed to obtain information.

Possible indicators of intelligence operations against your company

1. Competitors know about your new projects, confidential business, trade secrets and strategies.

2. Various enquiries are made by strangers such as 'students, researchers and others' about your company's secrets and new projects.

3. Repair technicians show up to do 'technical work' when no one has called them.

4. The same competitors regularly beat you in tenders and business contracts.

5. Electronic bugging or surveillance devices are discovered on your business premises.

6. There are constant foreign requests for information or for permission to visit your company or facility.

7. Competitors beat you to the market with new products looking very similar to your own new designs.

8. Confidential material, information and equipment such as laptops are stolen under suspicious circumstances.

9. Key staff leave your company to go and work for a competitor.

10. Staff reporting surveillance, recruitment attempts or suspicious enquiries and behaviour.

COUNTERINTELLIGENCE AND SECURITY

Counterintelligence should not be confused with security. Counterintelligence is directed at coping with threats against information and is slowly finding its own place in the business world as a discipline separate and distinct from traditional security practices.

Threats must be frequently reassessed. Many companies employ security or countermeasures that do not address most of the threats against business information.

The counterintelligence function should preferably be separate from the normal security functions in a company unless your security department possesses a deep understanding of your business, objectives, strategy and plans.

Competitors are also using sophisticated methods and intelligence principles which need similar sophisticated counterintelligence mechanisms and strategies that go far beyond the traditional security of gates, guards, dogs and alarms. At most these security measures will only provide protection against the most obvious and perhaps the less sophisticated attacks.

Only a few (depending on the size of the company) highly skilled and trusted individuals reporting to the company's CEO should staff the counterintelligence section or unit. Counterintelligence personnel should understand your competitors and your business, and also have knowledge of basic security principles and measures.

Security policies usually do not make provision for counterintelligence or reflect poor insight into counterintelligence matters. Security policies will not address issues such as whether a company publishes or make too much information available about itself.

Counterintelligence will protect secrets, frustrate attempts by rivals wanting to acquire your secrets and catch out the competitors conducting competitive intelligence operations against your company.

Examples of espionage and intelligence-gathering uncovered

The number of reported incidents reflects the fact that no industry is 'safe':

■ In early September 2001 the US company Procter & Gamble (P&G) blew the whistle on itself and admitted to a competitor, the Anglo-Dutch firm, Unilever, that it conducted intelligence operations against it. One of the contractors hired by P&G to collect information against Unilever engaged in dumpster diving, may have trespassed on Uniliver property and was rumoured to have misrepresented themselves. Both companies are in the multi-billion dollar global hair care business. (Fortune.com)

- During August 2001 Rafael Bravo a security guard at British Aerospace, was arrested for stealing documents which covered areas such as radars and attack helicopters designated as NATO secrets. (News & City)

- During August 2001 the FBI issued a warrant of arrest for Xingkin Wu. It is alleged that while he worked at Corning in the USA, he passed on trade secrets to a competing fibre-optics maker in China. (The Star.com)

- Towards the end of July 2001 Themba Khumalo, a general manager at MTN in South Africa, joined Cell C sparking high drama and panic over missing corporate secrets and a laptop computer. MTN's biggest concern was his knowledge of strategies to counter Cell C's entry into the market. Both companies are in the cellular telephone business. Cell C is a new entrant to the market. (*Sunday Times*)

- During July 2001 the Governor of the South African Reserve Bank, Tito Mboweni, admitted that bugs and listening devices were found in the Reserve Bank and that it appears that someone in London apparently benefited from the information (*Financial Mail*)

- During May 2001 Takashi Okamoto was charged in the USA with stealing trade secrets from the Cleveland Clinic Foundation regarding the role of genetics in causing Alzheimer's disease and passing it on to the Japanese Riken Brain Science Institute. (*US News*)

- During May 2001 Avant was fined US$27 million for trade secret misappropriation from Cadence. Four Cadence employees left the company and started Avant in direct competition with Cadence. It was alleged by Cadence that the four took Cadence's code for chip design software with them and used it in their own company. (*E-Company*)

- During March 2001 a food services worker at MasterCard International was arrested after he approached VISA with information about a confidential transaction between MasterCard and a large US entertainment company. (Counterintel-SA)

- During February 2001 Kraft's frozen pizza division decided to sue rival Schwan's for the alleged theft of trade secrets. An American private investigator, Mark Barry published the book *Spooked* in December 2000. In one of the chapters he alleged that he worked for Schwan's and through various unethical and other means obtained confidential information about a division of Kraft's which enabled Schwan's to gain a competitive edge.

THE ROLE AND FUNCTIONS OF
PASSIVE COUNTERINTELLIGENCE

Passive counterintelligence aims to counter what a competitor may do and comprises mostly preventative measures. These measures are also recommended for most companies.

It is better to prepare in advance against what a competitor can do than to deal with the information loss after it has occurred. This will minimize or prevent the success of potential actions by competitors.

The measures are not expensive to implement and will enhance efforts to protect sensitive and confidential information. Some of the measures are as follows:

- *Counterintelligence education* aims to heighten the awareness of personnel and alert them to the threats of business espionage and other dangers to information. Companies spend millions on computer firewalls, access control and other security barriers but few invest in awareness training for their staff. The best security systems will be useless if staff members are ignorant about the tactics and modus operandi employed to steal business secrets. Regular awareness training will improve staff's knowledge of the legal, unethical and illegal information-gathering techniques.

- *Defensive measures* include programmes aimed at identifying possible threats among personnel and monitoring those deemed vulnerable to outside coercion. An employee assistance programme (EAP) can become an important counterintelligence tool. Counterintelligence recognizes the link between personal problems and risks regarding the protection of information. The defensive measures should be able to help to identify those with the problems mentioned above and the EAP should be aimed at improving the well-being of the troubled staff member. The EAP offers counselling and other support to help people find solutions to the problems that distract them. Many times these problems also contribute to them becoming vulnerable for recruitment by an industrial spy.

- *Technical surveillance countermeasures (TSCM)* are a set of measures to identify hostile and illegal technical devices planted for information collection purposes. If all avenues to a company have been successfully cut off for the industrial spy he or she will turn to technology. This is not a new threat. Incidents of failed electronic espionage are regularly reported in the press. One of the earlier cases reported was that of Joseph Wiegers of McFadden's 'Publicity Department'. He was indicted on 5 December 1941 in the USA after he was trapped bugging a Fawcett's sales force convention in a Louisville Hotel. Fawcett Distribution Corporation was a competitor of McFadden's at the time.

  Major decisions are often made orally long before they are committed to writing. The audio surveillance of important meeting places and boardrooms where decisions are made can give the industrial spy not only the information required but also the lead time to make good use of the information. Products that were supposed to make our communications easier all have built-in vulnerabilities that could be exploited for electronic eavesdropping.

TSCM aims to prevent or to limit technical intrusions by any hostile entity. It is important to note that professionals utilizing appropriate equipment and techniques should conduct the technical surveillance countermeasures surveys. Regular TSCM surveys have become a standard business practice. The general accepted practice for corporate business is a quarterly inspection. The sensitivity level of the area will dictate if more or fewer inspections are required.

■ *Penetration testing* refers to the assessment of the vulnerabilities of sensitive facilities, areas and activities to outside attack. High-value commodities within the business environment are targeted on a daily basis by perpetrators attempting to penetrate facilities, systems or countermeasures to reach their aim. Where physical high-value commodities are involved the loss may be felt within a short time and directly linked to a specific incident that took place. When incidents of penetration take place to copy documents or other information or to gather information by electronic eavesdropping the loss may only be discovered long after the penetration has been perpetrated.

Most security systems cannot withstand an effective penetration effort by a professional espionage team. This is mainly due to a lack of properly conducted security and counterintelligence surveys and analysis of critical factors, system designs not tested in practice, the human factor, a low level of security and information protection consciousness, the absence of regular security auditing and the absence of penetration testing of implemented systems. Regular penetration testing will evaluate the effectiveness of the systems in place, improve overall security and limit opportunities for the industrial spy.

COUNTERINTELLIGENCE POLICIES AND PROCEDURES

Companies all have policies about such things as smoking, first aid, sexual harassment, drugs and alcohol abuse to name but a few, but many do not have policies regarding counterintelligence and the protection of information against industrial espionage and competitive intelligence. Most companies do not budget or allocate resources for the passive counterintelligence measures described above.

Effective counterintelligence policies and procedures will classify information and prescribe the handling of the information within the company. There are two requirements that have to be met before information can be classified as confidential. Only a limited number of people must know about the information and there should be a legal duty on them to keep that information confidential or secret.

The policies and procedures will also make provision for the pre-employment screening and integrity testing of those persons in a company entrusted with the company's confidential information. It will also make provision for non-disclosure and non-competitive agreements for certain employees to deter them from taking up employment with specified competitors within a stated future period.

The importance of counterintelligence procedures must not be underestimated. It will instil a culture and positive attitude regarding the protection of information.

CONCLUSION

Many companies mistakenly still believe that counterintelligence is not necessary, as they do not face any threats against their information. However, companies do need to allocate resources for the protection of information. By implementing counterintelligence as part of a company's strategy, management will strengthen the company's overall competitive position in the marketplace.

Counterintelligence is not a separate step in the intelligence process or cycle; rather, it is an essential function throughout the process and must be integrated with competitive intelligence. It will also strengthen and contribute to the overall security efforts.

As James A. Schweitzer puts it, in *Protecting Business Information: A Manager's Guide* (1996):

> *If one waits until a threat is manifest through a successful attack, then significant damage can be done before an effective countermeasure can be developed and deployed. Therefore countermeasures may be based on speculation. Efforts may be expended in countering attacks that are never attempted. The need to speculate and to budget resources for countermeasures also implies a need to understand what it is that should be protected, and why; such understanding should drive the choice of a protection strategy and countermeasures. This thinking should be captured in security policies generated by management; poor security often reflects both weak policies and inadequate forethought.*

Appendices

Interview with Ismo Rautiainen

Senior Vice President for Business Development,
Outokumpu Copper Products

Outokumpu Oyj is a global metals and technology group, originally incorporated in 1932 in the town in eastern Finland of the same name. Today its headquarters are in Espoo, just outside Helsinki. Group net sales for 2001 were approximately €5½bn, and at the end of 2001 the compnay's market capitalization stood at some €1bn. Outokumpu operates in three main business areas: (1) copper products, which represents about 27 per cent of sales; (2) metallurgy, which contributes about 21 per cent turnover; and (3) stainless steel – supplied by AvestaPolarit, a company formed in January 2001 by the merger OCP's stainless steel division and Avesta Sheffield – accounts for most of the remaining 53 per cent of revenues. The Finnish state owns 40 per cent of the company, but the government's stake is expected to be reduced to as little as 10 per cent subject to pending legislation.

The Outokumpu Copper Products Business Area (OCP) is the world's second largest produced in its industry in terms of volume, offering a wide range of essentially *specialty*-type products to customers worldwide. These include everything from radiator strips used for heat exchanges by the automotive industry, to superconductors for customers in the high-technology domain, to thin-walled tubes for air-conditioner and refrigeration equipment manufacturers. OCP, like its sister companies, is an 'old economy' player in an uncertain and competitive business environment. Nevertheless, the company believe that that there is no modern society without copper, and have therefore defined a strategic direction 'based on the fact that comfort and communication are driving the consumption of copper. In addition to volume the value of different solutions needed will be increasing even faster.' Historically its competitors tended to be regional rather than global firms, but this is now changing. Increasingly, OCP is competing against global players.

Business intelligence (BI) at OCP has a high profile and is the responsibility of the company's Senior Vice President for Business Development, Ismo Rautiainen. This is how he explains business intelligence at OCP:

> *The focus of BI at OCP is on strategic intelligence. The objective is to make the link between BI and the company's strategy. First, we try to identify the key strategic issues in our business environment; this enables us to gain management's attention, or recognition. We must therefore speak the 'language' of our internal customers, the top executives as well as decision 'influencers'.*

Our job is to tackle questions such as what are the fundamental drivers of our industry? We also believe that it's not enough to have only one 'vision' of the world; we consider possible worlds, and we monitor external developments to ensure that our vision is still working, and is still relevant. How should we as a company behave in the face of new external realities? Today, for example, about 70 per cent of copper usage is based on heat and electrical conductivity applications. Will this continue to be the case?

Some of the main topics we address include:

- Customers – *in particular those in the automotive, electrical power generation, and information technology sectors, including telecommunications. What is the impact of wireless communications on our industry? Does this mean diminishing requirements for copper cable? If we believed that copper consumption will decrease, this would have a profound influence on our future strategies. What are new applications, and maybe new customer segments, for copper in a mobile world? Can we determine this faster and with greater actionable insight than the competition? What are the views of our rivals in this regard?*

- Globalization – *how should we behave toward customers who say they are global, but act regionally (local)? How do we assess regionally based information and indicators in a global context?*

- De-regulation.

- The accelerating convergence between information technology and telecommunications – *especially the tension which exists between open and proprietary standards; this also represents a conflict between different industry cultures.*

Business intelligence is important to us at OCP for many reasons:

- *Because the dynamics of future growth areas are increasingly volatile, we feel a greater need than ever before to 'understand' the future. For example, when will third-generation mobile communications start driving copper consumption for network infrastructures? This involves understanding our customers' customers as well as emerging new business mobiles and value chains.*

- *If management are to lead the organization – and this, as far as I am concerned, is their principal responsibility – strategic intelligence will become increasingly necessary for success ... how can you take decisions about the game if you don't understand the playing field? Indeed, we believe the main challenge for strategic intelligence is to help us answer the question: what is the right business concept for the future? How, in* one sense, can we help provide management with the courage they need to move forward?

■ Business intelligence also helps us determine what segments we don't wish to serve. For example, we do not supply brass or wire rod.

■ It helps us think about the match between our strategic intent and our resource allocation and product portfolio decisions. For example, what do we need to know to better consider the decision: do we want to remain in profitable businesses with little growth prospects? Should we consider alternative products? Or will we suffer from the threats of substitute products? Unfortunately, operational and sales managers are often 'blind' to changing realities; they become married to their specific operational activities. Strategic intelligence helps us overcome this problem.

At present, our BI team at OCP is small – three persons. Our brief is to support the CEO and top management, although we continue to receive more and more requests, on different subjects, form an expanding array of managers. Our dialogue with our top management is getting better and better. In addition, there is a need for different intelligence sub-processes in different phases of the company's strategy process. Unfortunately, I'm not at liberty to elaborate on this point.

Regardless of how 'good' the intelligence we produce is, it's interesting to note that our executives traditionally use external sources to support their information needs – their own network of contacts mainly – to 'check' the reliability of the intelligence we deliver. Indeed, we're increasingly challenged by management's greater expectations from intelligence, partly as a result of its increasing visibility in the company, although we always remember that it's not the job of intelligence to make decisions; we're there to deliver evidence and analysis. Management are concerned with opportunities for profitable growth and threats to that growth. It's also important to note that we encourage executives to challenge our intelligence findings and analysis. This stimulates healthy debate.

In my view, strategic intelligence must help management better understand the world outside the company but not to interfere with the decisions of business managers. Intelligence must be marketed, and must be persuasive. At times, we use management's existing information to support our findings. Being too research-oriented – or data driven – doesn't produce intelligence that's worth much. Our aim is to use strategic intelligence to ain competitive advantage, but it must be properly understood and applied by management. This means we must continuously test existing assumptions. Dissemination formats, too, must be kept simple, or the information and its implications *just won't by understood. Strategic management involves connecting, or integrating, intelligence with the strategy process. At the Outokumpu corporate level, however, management still have some way to go toward improving its willingness to listen to industry and market signals.*

I think, too, the effectiveness of intelligence is, perhaps, a function of the openness of a company's culture; otherwise, one's arguments tend not to carry more weight than their organizational rank.

Interview with Neil Mahoney

Formerly Vice President and Head of Global Intelligence,
Novartis International AG

Novartis International AG, based in Basel, Switzerland, is one of the world's largest pharmaceutical companies, numbering some 71,000 employees at the end of the 2001 financial year. Forged in the mid-1990s in the merger of Ciba-Geigy and Sandoz, total group sales for 2001 were approximately US$19 billion, of which its pharmaceuticals sector accounted for over 60 per cent. At the beginning of 2002 its market capitalization was approximately $90 billion. In addition to its pharmaceuticals business, the company's other divisions include Consumer Health, Generics, CIBA Vision and Animal Health. The company's strategic objectives call for a continuing focus on healthcare and pharmaceuticals as its core business. Key product sectors in pharmaceuticals include primary care, oncology, ophthalmics and transplantation.

Let me describe what competitive intelligence [CI] means at Novartis. The starting point as far as I am concerned is strategy, which I define as 'the science of planning and the skill in managing an operation to gain and sustain an advantage over competitors'. The components of strategic planning at Novartis are illustrated in Figure A2.1.

Fig. A2.1 Components of strategic planning at Novartis

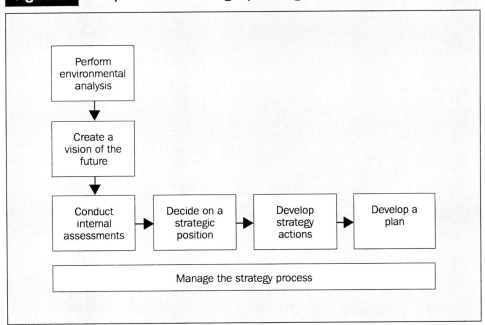

At Novartis, CI supports each phase of the process at all levels: group, sector, business unit and country/market. This means we're concerned with issues involving the industry, specific companies and products.

When, for example, we perform environmental analysis, we tend to focus on industry dynamics and players, competitor pipeline developments and their likely impact on our own business, and scientific and technological advances.

Our strategy focus, of course, differs at the various levels mentioned. At the group level, we are mainly concerned with our portfolio of businesses: looking over ten years, how should we change our portfolio? At the sector level, say Pharmaceuticals, we are concerned mainly with questions regarding our product portfolio, such as what is the right mix of franchises between mass market or niche segments, as an example. At the business unit level we focus on topics such as therapeutic area selection and current product portfolio management. At the country/market level our principal, and shorter term, concerns centre around optimization of the local product portfolio.

When targeting a specific competitor, typically we would want answers to questions regarding the whats, whens, whys and hows of organizational structure, field force (sales) operations, research and development decision processes, and product pipelines.

What do we consider are the key features of CI? There are four that spring to mind:

1. *A focus on the future competitive environment. It's too late to do anything about what's happening today, and certainly yesterday!*

2. *CI must deal with issues across the whole of a firm's 'business chain'.*

3. *CI often deals with, and must make sense of, 'soft' information. This is a tough call for those who are 'numbers oriented'.*

4. *Scenario-building based on limited facts. There is, after all, no data on the future.*

You asked what we see as the essential functional responsibilities of CI. These are what are important to us at Novartis:

■ *support for the strategy process;*

■ *assessment and monitoring of key competitors;*

■ *support for tactical implementation of strategic plans;*

■ *early warning of competitive threats and opportunities.*

I'm often asked to make comparisons between the respective roles of CI and market research. I can answer that question in one short table [Table A2.1].

Table A2.1 Competitive intelligence vs. market research

Competitive intelligence	Market research
Future view	Present view
Business chain	Market focus
Soft information	Facts and opinions
Scenario-building	Segmentation

And yes, we have a CI Mission Statement. It reads thus:

> *'Our mission is to collect, analyse, and disseminate unbiased intelligence relative to the strategic interests, objectives, and priorities of Novartis.'*

Last, a few points regarding the role that the Corporate CI group is responsible for with Novartis:

Corporate CI

■ *Support Corporate's strategic needs.*

■ *Establish systems to build internal CI networks.*

■ *Establish processes to develop the function.*

■ *Help prevent intellectual asset loss.*

■ *Support sector CI units.*

■ *Establish CI policy and procedures.*

■ *Define ethical and legal guidelines.*

■ *Provide training support.*

■ *Share 'best practices' across sectors.*

■ *Monitor sector compliance with established policies.*

The impact of CI can be quite profound. Consider the difference having the right intelligence, at the right time, and at the following levels of focus, has made to us:

Industry level

■ *Industry analysis of top players over the next five years helped us develop our M&A [mergers and acquisitions] strategy. Our CI team specifically helped eliminate unsuitable candidates for M&A and BD&L [business development and licensing] deals through confidential pre-screening.*

■ *Environmental assessment for Primary Care disease strategy. Intelligence, here, was instrumental in future portfolio selection focusing BD&L and research efforts.*

Issue level

Competitive benchmarking studies were key influences for Pharma strategies in biotechnology, managed care, generics, and R&D structure.

Product level

■ *Competitive pipeline monitoring used to adjust Phase III/IV programmes to improve marketing profile upon launch against competitive products.*

■ *Generic monitoring used in lifecycle management to improve resource allocation resulting in higher revenues and EBITs [earnings before interest and taxation] on several key brands.*

I'll conclude with the following points:

■ *CI has proven its value to senior management over the past few decades and so has become an accepted 'profession' within most corporate organizations.*

■ *The field will continue to grow as it provides the external view needed to optimize strategic resource allocation related to business and product portfolios.*

■ *CI should be part of every planning process from the local sales operation level to the global strategic level in order to ensure that management has the best opportunity to make informed decisions regarding managing the corporate assets to maximize shareholder value.*

References

Ashton, W.B. and Klavans, R.A. (eds) (1997) *Keeping Abreast of Science and Technology: Technical Intelligence for Business*. Columbus, OH: Battelle Press.

ASIS/PwC LLP (1999) *Trends in Proprietary Information Loss*, Survey Report. ASIS/PricewaterhouseCoopers LLP.

Baumard, P. (1994) 'From noticing to making sense: using intelligence to develop strategy', *International Journal of Intelligence and Counterintelligence*, 7, 1: 37.

Belkine, M. (ed.) (2001) 'Corporate CI – tactical or strategic?', *Competitive Intelligence Magazine*, September–October: 27–31.

Berkowitz, B.D. and Goodman, A.E. (1989) *Strategic Intelligence for American National Security*. Princeton: NJ: Princeton University Press.

Bernhardt, D.C. (1999) *Competitive Intelligence in Pharmaceuticals: The Strategic Advantage*. London: Vision in Business.

CIA (2002a) *DI Analytic Toolkit*. Available at http://www.cia.gov/cia/di/toolkit/index.html [accessed 9 September 2002].

CIA (2002b) *Analytic Toolkit: Addressing US Interests in DI Assessments*. Available at: http://www.cia.gov/cia/di/toolkit/index.html [accessed 9 September 2002].

Colby, W. (1978) *Honourable Men: My Life in the CIA*. London: Hutchinson.

Corporate Strategy Board (2000) *Strategic Intelligence: Providing Critical Information for Strategic Decisions*. Washington, DC: Corporate Strategy Board.

Coyne, K.P. (2000) 'Sustainable competitive advantage', *McKinsey Quarterly*, 3: 31–4.

d'Aveni, R.A. (2001) *Strategic Supremacy: How Industry Leaders Create Growth, Wealth, and Power through Spheres of Influence*. New York: Free Press.

Fleisher, C.S. and Bensoussan, B.E. (2002) *Strategic and Competitive Analysis: Methods and Techniques for Analysing Business Competition*. Upper Saddle River, NJ: Prentice Hall.

Ford, H.P. (1993) *Estimative Intelligence*. McLean, VA: Association of Former Intelligence Officers.

Gardiner, L.K. (1989) 'Dealing with intelligence policy disconnects', *Studies in Intelligence*, 33, 2: 1–9.

Gates, R.M. (1987/88) 'The CIA and American foreign policy', *Foreign Affairs*, Winter: 215–30.

Gilad, B. (1991) 'US intelligence system: model for corporate chiefs?', *Journal of Business Strategy*, May/June: 20–5.

Gilad, B. (1994) *Business Blindspots*. Chicago: Probus.

Grabo, C.M. (1987) *Warning Intelligence*. McLean, VA: Association of Former Intelligence Officers.

Hamel, G. (2000) *Leading the Revolution*. Boston, MA: Harvard Business School Press.

Hamel, G. and Prahalad, C.K. (1994) *Competing for the Future*. Boston, MA: Harvard Business School Press.

Hamilton, P. (1979) *Espionage, Terrorism and Subversion in an Industrial Society*. Leatherhead, Surrey: Peter A. Heims.

Handel, M.I. (1989) *War, Strategy and Intelligence*. London: Frank Cass.

Herman, M. (1996) *Intelligence Power in Peace and War*. Cambridge: Cambridge University Press.

Herring, J.P. (1996) 'Creating the intelligence system that produces analytical intelligence' in Gilad, B. and Herring, J.P. (eds.) *The Art and Science of Business Intelligence Analysis*, Part A. Greenwich, CT: JAI Press, 53–81.

Herring, J.P. (1999) *Key Intelligence Topics: A Process to Identify and Define Intelligence Needs*. Hartford, CT: Jan P. Herring & Associates.

Herring, J.P. (1999) 'KITs revisited: their use and problems', *SCIP.online*, 1, 8, available at http://www.imakenews.com/scip2/e_article000069099.cfm?x=108456,4234443.

Hoge Jr, J.F. and Rose, G. (2001) *How Did This Happen: Terrorism and the New War*. Oxford: PublicAffairs.

Hussey, D. and Jenster, P. (1999) *Competitor Intelligence: Turning Analysis into Success*. Chichester: John Wiley & Sons.

Kahn, D. (2001) 'A historical theory of intelligence', *Intelligence and National Security*, 16, 3 (Autumn).

Kovaks, A. (1997) 'Using intelligence', *Intelligence and National Security*, 12(4) 145–64.

Krizan, L. (1999) *Intelligence Essentials for Everyone*. Washington, DC: Joint Military Intelligence College.

Matthias, W.C. (2001) *America's Strategic Blunders*. University Park, PA: Pennsylvania State University Press.

Office of Homeland Security (2002) *National Strategy for Homeland Security*. Washington, DC: The White House.

Office of Public Affairs (1999) *A Consumer's Guide to Intelligence*. Washington, DC: Central Intelligence Agency.

Pappas, A.A. and Simon Jr, J.M. (2002) 'The intelligence community: 2000–2015', *Studies in Intelligence*, 46, 1, available online at http://www.cia.gov/csi/studies/vol46no1/article05.html.

Porter, M.E. (1980) *Competitive Strategy: Techniques for Analysing Industries and Competitors*. New York: Free Press.

Porter, M.E. (2000) *Industry Transformation*, Harvard Business School Note 701-008.

Sawka, K.A. and Fiora, B. (1997) *Early Warning Analysis: Advanced Issues*. Glastonbury, CT: Futures Group.

Schweitzer, J.A. (1996) *Protecting Business Information: A Manager's Guide*. Newton, MA: Butterworth Heinemann.

SCIP (1997) *Navigating through the Gray Zone*. Alexandria, VA: Society of Competitive Intelligence Professionals.

Sharer, K. (1990) 'Top management's intelligence needs: an executive's view of competitive intelligence', in SCIP (ed.), *Fall Conference*, Chicago, October. Alexandria, VA: Society of Competitive Intelligence Professionals.

Sulc, L.B. (1996) *Law Enforcement Counterintelligence*. Shawnee Mission, KS: Varro Press.

Treverton, G.F. (2001) *Reshaping National Intelligence for an Age of Information*. Cambridge: Cambridge University Press.

United States Subcommittee on Terrorism and Homeland Security, House Permanent Select Committee on Intelligence (2002) *Counterterrorism Intelligence Capabilities and Performance prior to 9-11: A Report to the Speaker of the House of Representatives and the Minority Leader*. Washington, DC: House of Representatives, July.

Wright, P., Pringle, C. and Kroll, M. (1992) *Strategic Management Text and Cases*. Needham Heights, MA: Allyn & Bacon.

Zuehlke, Jr., A.A. and Miller, N.S. (1980) 'Counterintelligence', in Godson, R. (ed.) *Intelligence Requirements for the 1980s*. 7 vols. Washington DC: National Strategy Information Center, 1979–85.